UNITED NATIONS CONFERENCE ON TRADE AND DEVELOPMENT

NATIONAL TREATMENT

UNCTAD Series
on issues in international investment agreements

UNITED NATIONS
New York and Geneva, 1999

NOTE

DB# 1582525

UNCTAD serves as the focal point within the United Nations Secretariat for all matters related to foreign direct investment and transnational corporations. In the past, the Programme on Transnational Corporations was carried out by the United Nations Centre on Transnational Corporations (1975-1992) and the Transnational Corporations and Management Division of the United Nations Department of Economic and Social Development (1992-1993). In 1993, the Programme was transferred to the United Nations Conference on Trade and Development. UNCTAD seeks to further the understanding of the nature of transnational corporations and their contribution to development and to create an enabling environment for international investment and enterprise development. UNCTAD's work is carried out through intergovernmental deliberations, research and analysis, technical assistance activities, seminars, workshops and conferences.

The term "country" as used in this study also refers, as appropriate, to territories or areas; the designations employed and the presentation of the material do not imply the expression of any opinion whatsoever on the part of the Secretariat of the United Nations concerning the legal status of any country, territory, city or area or of its authorities, or concerning the delimitation of its frontiers or boundaries. In addition, the designations of country groups are intended solely for statistical or analytical convenience and do not necessarily express a judgement about the stage of development reached by a particular country or area in the development process.

The following symbols have been used in the tables:

Two dots (..) indicate that data are not available or are not separately reported. Rows in tables have been omitted in those cases where no data are available for any of the elements in the row;

A dash (-) indicates that the item is equal to zero or its value is negligible;

A blank in a table indicates that the item is not applicable;

A slash (/) between dates representing years, e.g. 1994/95, indicates a financial year;

Use of a hyphen (-) between dates representing years, e.g. 1994-1995, signifies the full period involved, including the beginning and end years.

Reference to "dollars" ($) means United States dollars, unless otherwise indicated.

Annual rates of growth or change, unless otherwise stated, refer to annual compound rates.

Details and percentages in tables do not necessarily add to totals because of rounding.

The material contained in this study may be freely quoted with appropriate acknowledgement.

UNCTAD/ITE/IIT/11 (Vol. IV)

UNITED NATIONS PUBLICATION

Sales No. E.99.II.D.16

ISBN 92-1-112455-7

UN2
ii

TD/UNCTAD/ITE/IIT/11 (Vol.IV)

IIA Issues Paper Series

The main purpose of the UNCTAD Series on issues in international investment agreements is to address key concepts and issues relevant to international investment agreements and to present them in a manner that is easily accessible to end-users. The series covers the following topics:

Admission and establishment
Competition
Dispute settlement (investor-State)
Dispute settlement (State-State)
Employment
Environment
Fair and equitable treatment
Foreign direct investment and development
Funds transfer
Home country measures
Host country operational measures
Illicit payments
Incentives
Investment-related trade measures
Lessons from the Uruguay Round
Modalities and implementation issues
Most-favoured-nation treatment
National treatment
Present international arrangements for foreign direct investment:
    an overview
Scope and definition
Social responsibility
State contracts
Taking of property
Taxation
Transfer of technology
Transfer pricing
Transparency

Preface

The United Nations Conference on Trade and Development (UNCTAD) is implementing a work programme on a possible multilateral framework on investment, with a view towards assisting developing countries to participate as effectively as possible in international investment rule-making at the bilateral, regional, plurilateral and multilateral levels. The programme embraces capacity-building seminars, regional symposia, training courses, dialogues between negotiators and groups of civil society and the preparation of a series of issues papers.

This paper is part of this series. It is addressed to government officials, corporate executives, representatives of non-governmental organizations, officials of international agencies and researchers. The series seeks to provide balanced analyses of issues that may arise in discussions about international investment agreements. Each study may be read by itself, independently of the others. Since, however, the issues treated closely interact with one another, the studies pay particular attention to such interactions.

The series is produced by a team led by Karl P. Sauvant and Pedro Roffe. The principal officer responsible for its production is John Gara who oversees the development of the papers at various stages. The other members of the team include Obiajulu Ihonor and Jörg Weber. The work is carried out under the overall direction of Lynn K. Mytelka. The series' principal advisors are Arghyrios A. Fatouros, Sanjaya Lall and Peter T. Muchlinski. Drawing on a first draft by Patrick Robinson, the present paper is based on a manuscript prepared by Peter T. Muchlinski. Victoria Aranda was responsible for the substantive supervision of this paper. The final version reflects comments received from Joachim Karl, Mark Koulen, Hamid Mamdouh and Marinus Sikkel. The paper was desktop published by Teresita Sabico.

Rubens Ricupero
Secretary-General of UNCTAD

Geneva, May 1999

Acknowledgments

UNCTAD's work programme on a possible multilateral framework on investment is implemented by a team of UNCTAD staff members and consultants headed by Karl P. Sauvant and Pedro Roffe and including Victoria Aranda, Mattheo Bushehri, Ruvan de Alwis, Arghyrios A. Fatouros, John Gara, Obiajulu Ihonor, Anna Joubin-Bret, Sanjaya Lall, Peter T. Muchlinski, Miguel Rodriguez and Jörg Weber. Administrative support is provided by Christiane Defrancisco and Antonia Künzel.

UNCTAD has carried out a number of activities related to the work programme in cooperation with other intergovernmental organizations, including the Secretariat of the Andean Community, the Inter-Arab Investment Guarantee Corporation, the League of Arab States, the Organization of American States, l'Organisation Internationale de la Francophonie, and the World Trade Organization. UNCTAD has also cooperated with non-governmental organizations, including the Centro de Estudios Interdisciplinarios de Derecho Industrial y Económico - Universidad de Buenos Aires, the Consumer Unity and Trust Society - India, the Economic Research Forum - Cairo, the European Roundtable of Industrialists, the Friedrich Ebert Foundation, the International Confederation of Free Trade Unions, Oxfam, SOMO - Centre for Research on Multinational Corporations, the Third World Network, Universidad del Pacifico, University of the West Indies, and World Wildlife Fund International.

Funds for the work programme have so far been received from Australia, Brazil, Canada, France, the Netherlands, Norway, Switzerland, the United Kingdom and the European Commission. Countries such as Egypt, India, Jamaica, Morocco and Peru have also contributed to the work programme by hosting regional symposia. All of these contributions are gratefully acknowledged.

Table of contents

Executive summary

The national treatment standard is perhaps the single most important standard of treatment enshrined in international investment agreements (IIAs). At the same time, it is perhaps the most difficult standard to achieve, as it touches upon economically (and politically) sensitive issues. In fact, no single country has so far seen itself in a position to grant national treatment without qualifications, especially when it comes to the establishment of an investment.

National treatment can be defined as a principle whereby a host country extends to foreign investors treatment that is at least as favourable as the treatment that it accords to national investors in like circumstances. In this way the national treatment standard seeks to ensure a degree of competitive equality between national and foreign investors. This raises difficult questions concerning the factual situations in which national treatment applies and the precise standard of comparison by which the treatment of national and foreign investors is to be compared.

National treatment typically extends to the post-entry treatment of foreign investors. However, some bilateral investment treaties (BITs) and other IIAs also extend the standard to pre-entry situations. This has raised the question of the proper limits of national treatment, in that such an extension is normally accompanied by a "negative list" of excepted areas of investment activity to which national treatment does not apply, or a "positive list" of areas of investment activity to which national treatment is granted. In addition, several types of general exceptions to national treatment exist concerning public health, safety and morals, and national security, although these may not be present in all agreements, particularly not in BITs.

National treatment interacts with several other investment issues and concepts. Most notably there are strong interactions with the issues of admission and establishment, the most-favoured-nation (MFN) standard, host country operational measures and investor-State dispute settlement.

National treatment raises some of the most significant development issues in the field of foreign direct investment (FDI). It stipulates formal equality between foreign and national investors. However, in practice national investors, especially those that could be identified as "infant industries" or "infant entrepreneurs", may be in an economically disadvantageous position by comparison with foreign investors, who may be economically powerful transnational corporations (TNCs). Such "economic asymmetry" may require a degree of flexibility in the treatment of national investors, especially in developing countries, for instance through the granting of exceptions to national treatment.

INTRODUCTION

The national treatment standard is one of the main general standards that is used in international practice to secure a certain level of treatment for FDI in host countries. Other general standards include principally, fair and equitable treatment (UNCTAD, 1999a) and MFN treatment (UNCTAD, 1999b). National treatment is a contingent standard based on the treatment given to other investors. Thus, while MFN seeks to grant foreign investors treatment comparable to other foreign investors operating in the host country, national treatment seeks to grant treatment comparable to domestic investors operating in the host country.

For many countries, the standard of national treatment serves to eliminate distortions in competition and thus is seen to enhance the efficient operation of the economies involved. An extension of this argument points to the ongoing internationalization of investment and production and concludes that access to foreign markets under non-discriminatory conditions is necessary for the effective functioning of an increasingly integrated world economy. On the other hand, there may be no substitute for the promotion by host countries of domestic industries to ensure economic development and, in a world marked by stark inequalities in economic power, technical capabilities and financial strength, a certain differentiation between national and non-national firms may be necessary precisely in order to bring about a degree of operative equality.

As will be discussed further in section I, national treatment is a relative standard whose content depends on the underlying state of treatment for domestic and foreign investors alike. It is also a standard that has its origins primarily in trade treaties, though, as noted below, the term has also been used in a quite different context, namely in relation to the customary international law standards for the treatment of aliens and their property. A certain degree of adaptation of the standard to the characteristics of investment is therefore required so that it may be used in an effective way in IIAs.

In the context of foreign investment relations, until relatively recently, national treatment was seen to be relevant almost exclusively to the treatment accorded to foreign investors after they had entered a host country. However, some more recent IIAs particularly the BITs entered into by Canada and the United States (apart from the Friendship Commerce and Navigation (FCN) treaties of the United States), have extended national treatment to the pre-entry stage so as to ensure market access for foreign investors on terms equal to those enjoyed by national investors. As national treatment traditionally applied in most BITs only to the post-establishment phase of an investment, and there was little question that the pre-establishment phase was left to the sovereign right of States in terms of deciding on admission of an investment (UNCTAD, 1999c), the extension of national treatment from the post- to the pre-investment phase is a "revolution"[1] for many countries. This has made the discussions about the type and extent of exceptions to national treatment that may be required in order to retain a measure of host country discretion in investment matters all the more important. In particular, as will be considered in sections I and II below, there may be a choice between granting a general right to national treatment subject to a "negative list" of excepted industries and areas to which national treatment does not apply, and proceeding on the basis of a "positive list" where no a priori general right to national treatment is granted and national treatment extends only to those industries and areas specifically included in the positive list. The development implications of these alternatives are discussed in the concluding section.

The substantive test of differential treatment takes up much of the discussion in section II. Here there are a significant number of alternatives. Thus, the factual area to which national treatment applies may be limited only to the "same" or "identical" situations, or it may be delimited by reference to a list of economic activities, or by reference to "like" or "similar" cases or circumstances. Some agreements are silent on this issue, leaving it up to the parties to determine on a case-by-case basis whether national treatment applies to a particular situation. Once the factual area of application has been determined, the next question is that of comparing the treatment offered to national and foreign investors. This may require that the treatment be the "same as" or "as favourable as" that accorded to national investors, or that it be "no less favourable", the latter offering the possibility not only of equal treatment but also of better treatment for foreign investors where this is deemed appropriate.

Given the significance of national treatment for development, some countries may find it hard to give up their power to treat foreign and domestic investors differently. Thus, in certain rare cases IIAs are silent on national treatment. However, in the majority of recent IIAs national treatment is present. As will be shown particularly in section II and the concluding section, the inclusion of national treatment may be done in such a way as to preserve a high level of host country authority or in a way that ensures a high standard of treatment for foreign investors. Alternatively, a hybrid approach may be taken. Through the judicious use of qualifications and exceptions to national treatment, a balance can be struck between host country authority and the treatment of investors. In particular, the development needs of a developing country may require such flexibility in an agreement. How this can be achieved will be discussed in the concluding section.

Note

1   To quote Patrick Juillard, at a lecture on "Measures relating to the entry and establishment of investments", UNCTAD/WTO, Third Seminar on Investment, Trade and Economic Development, Evian-les-Bains, 21-22 April 1999.

Section I

EXPLANATION OF THE ISSUE

A. The nature and origins of the national treatment standard

One of the principal characteristics of the national treatment standard is its relativity. Given that the standard invites a comparison in the treatment accorded to foreign and domestic investors, this makes a determination of its content dependent on the treatment offered by a host country to domestic investors and not on some *a priori* absolute principles of treatment.

In international law, the national treatment standard has been invoked in two different contexts. In one context, the standard represents one of the competing international law doctrines for the treatment of the person and property of aliens which has come to be known as the "Calvo doctrine". Under this doctrine, which was supported especially by Latin American countries, aliens and their property are entitled only to the same treatment accorded to nationals of the host country under its national laws. In contrast with this doctrine, the doctrine of State responsibility for injuries to aliens and their property, which historically has been supported by developed countries, asserts that customary international law establishes a minimum international standard of treatment to which aliens are entitled, allowing for treatment more favourable than that accorded to nationals where this falls below the international minimum standard.[1]

In treaty practice, national treatment has its origins in trade agreements. The first treaties to apply a concept of non-differentiation between foreign and local traders can be traced back to the practices of the Hanseatic League in the twelfth and thirteenth centuries

(VerLoren van Themaat, 1981, pp. 16 ff). More recently, United States FCN treaties included a clause offering national treatment (Jackson, 1997, p. 397). Equally, national treatment has been a long-standing standard in patent and copyright conventions. Article 2 of the Paris Convention for the Protection of Industrial Property (1883) sanctions the principle that nationals of the member countries "shall have the same protection" as nationals of the host member country in which protection for intellectual property right is sought (United Nations, 1972, p. 313).

In trade matters, national treatment of imported products with respect to internal measures is one of the basic principles of the multilateral trading system created by the General Agreement on Tariffs and Trade (GATT). At least as originally negotiated in 1947, the primary focus of the GATT was on the control and liberalization of border measures restricting international trade in goods. A fundamental principle in this respect is that, as a general rule, any border measures designed to give a competitive advantage to domestic products should take the form of customs tariffs imposed at the border, and that the level of such customs tariffs should be a matter for negotiation and binding in national schedules. Within this scheme of things, article III of the GATT ("National Treatment on Internal Taxation and Regulation") plays a critical role since, as its paragraph 1 makes clear, it is designed to ensure that "internal" measures are not applied to imported or domestic products so as to afford protection to domestic production. It thus serves the purpose of ensuring that internal measures are not used to nullify or impair the effect of tariff concessions and other multilateral rules applicable to border measures. The role of the national treatment principle of GATT article III must therefore be understood in light of the distinction between border measures and internal measures.

In relation to FDI, national treatment involves an economic aim not dissimilar to that which has motivated its adoption in trade agreements: foreign and domestic investors should be subject to the same competitive conditions on the host country market, and therefore no government measure should unduly favour domestic investors.[2] However, because the distinction made in the field of trade in goods between border measures and internal measures has no meaningful equivalent in the field of investment, national treatment clauses in IIAs differ in scope and purpose from the national treatment principle of GATT article III. In particular, a key question arising in regard to the scope of application of national treatment in investment agreements is whether the principle applies to all phases of an investment, i.e. whether it applies only to the treatment of foreign investment after its entry, or whether it also applies to the entry of foreign investment.

Initially, the standard was thought not to be pertinent to entry issues, on the ground that countries have a sovereign right, well established in international law (UNCTAD, 1999c), to control the entry of aliens. In addition, a foreign investor, being "outside" the host country, was not in a similar or comparable position to the domestic investor, so that national treatment was not seen to make sense. Yet the extension of national treatment to the pre-entry phase, starting with United States FCN treaties, and, more recently, in United States and Canadian BITs [3] and the North American Free Trade Agreement (NAFTA)[4], may begin to change the approach to this issue. (See further, UNCTAD, 1999c.)

The scope of national treatment in the investment field goes well beyond its use in trade agreements. In particular, the reference to "products" in article III of the GATT is inadequate for investment agreements in that it restricts national treatment to trade in goods. The activities of foreign investors in their host countries encompass a wide array of operations, including international trade in products, trade in components, know-how and technology, local production and distribution, the raising of finance capital and the provision of services, not to mention the range of transactions involved in the creation and administration of a business enterprise. Hence wider categories of economic transactions may be subjected to national treatment disciplines under investment agreements than under trade agreements.

The principal beneficiaries of national treatment are "investors" and "investments". The scope and definitions of these terms are the subject of a separate paper in this series and will not be discussed in detail here (UNCTAD, 1999d). In the context of a national treatment provision, the question of whether the beneficiaries of the standard are foreign investors only or include also foreign investments can have important practical implications.

B. Principal issues

Principal issues arising from the application of the national treatment standard in IIAs to be discussed in greater detail later in this paper include the following:

1. Scope and application

The question of the scope of application of the national treatment standard involves two separate issues: first, at what stage of the investment process does national treatment apply; secondly, what is the meaning of national treatment where States have subnational authorities exercising constitutional powers to make investment policy?

The first issue involves consideration of whether national treatment applies to both the pre- and post-entry stages of the investment process or whether the national treatment standard applies only to investments that have already been admitted to a host country.

As to the second issue, there is little doubt that under international law the host country Government has the duty (irrespective of the pecularities of its constitutional system) to ensure the observance of national treatment commitments (as well as other international commitments) by all its subnational authorities, unless it is otherwise agreed. However, questions arise where subnational entities enjoy constitutional powers that may affect the treatment of a foreign investor. A question that may arise in this respect is: what category of national investors constitutes the criterion for comparison with foreign investors for the purpose of national treatment -- local subnational investors or other national investors? Further issues arise in relation to non-governmental self-regulatory organizations that undertake regulatory functions in many industries. Should such bodies be subject to national treatment disciplines and, if so, how?

2. The substantive content of the national treatment standard

This issue involves two closely related questions: first, what are the factual situations in which national treatment applies? Second, in what manner, and to what extent, is the treatment of foreign investors assimilated to that of nationals? The first issue defines the limits of factual comparison, while the second issue deals with the techniques of comparison, the application of which is limited to the factual situations identified in answering the first question.

3. The relationship between national treatment and other general standards of treatment

National treatment may co-exist in an IIA with other standards of treatment, notably MFN and fair and equitable treatment. This raises the technical question of how the relevant clauses relate to one another. National treatment may be stated in a "stand alone" provision or it may be combined with other general standards of treatment. It is common practice in IIAs to combine national treatment with MFN (less commonly with fair and equitable treatment) in one clause (UNCTAD, 1999a, 1999b). The main effect of such combinations is to emphasize the close interaction between the various standards of treatment. This may be supplemented by a further clause which entitles the foreign investor to the better of national treatment or MFN, whichever is more advantageous (and, in some cases, may result in treatment for foreign investors that is better than national treatment and therefore discriminates against local investors). Thus, for example, if a foreign investor received better treatment under an MFN clause than under a national treatment standard, the former would apply. This may be the case in situations in which some foreign investors already enjoy preferential treatment in a host country vis-à-vis national firms regarding, for example, incentives.

4. *"De jure"* and *"de facto"* treatment

A question that arises is whether national treatment covers not only *de jure* treatment, that is, treatment of foreign investors provided for in national laws and regulations, but also *de facto* treatment, as where a measure in fact works against national treatment. One example may be licensing requirements for the conduct of a certain business activity which depend on the possession of qualifications by skilled personnel that can only be obtained in the host country. Although this measure may be justifiable on policy grounds, as where health and safety issues are involved, it would require a foreign investor to ensure that its own personnel have the relevant national qualifications, requiring additional time and cost to be incurred before the investor can begin to operate.

5. Exceptions to national treatment

The use of exceptions enables host countries to exclude certain types of enterprises, activities or industries from the operation of national treatment. These may consist of:

- **General exceptions** based on reasons of public health, order and morals, and national security. Such exceptions are present in most regional and multilateral investment agreements, and also in a number of BITs.

- **Subject-specific exceptions** which exempt specific issues from national treatment, such as intellectual property, taxation provisions in bilateral tax treaties, prudential measures in financial services or temporary macroeconomic safeguards.

- **Country-specific exceptions** whereby a contracting party reserves the right to differentiate between domestic and foreign investors under its laws and regulations -- in particular, those related to specific industries or activities -- for reasons of national economic and social policy.

The number and scope of exceptions determines the practical effect of national treatment under an investment agreement.

Another issue related to the question of exceptions is whether the standard is based on reciprocity of treatment between the home and host countries of an investor. Some provisions have made national treatment conditional upon the reciprocal granting of national treatment to investors of all contracting parties to an IIA, while others retain a non-reciprocal commitment to the standard.

Notes

1   For a detailed analysis of the concepts and principles of customary international law applying to foreign investment, see UNCTC, 1990a; Fatouros, 1993, and UNCTAD, 1998b.

2   However, the rationale for the granting of national treatment varies, depending on the economic sectors and the subject matter involved. Thus, in a certain sense, the assimilation of aliens and nationals may be seen as forming part of international protection and the promotion of human rights, as far as basic standards of treatment of the person and property are concerned (e.g. protection against arbitrary government action, guarantees of human rights). This rationale may or may not extend beyond the treatment of the person to touch upon property rights and the rights of legal persons (UNCTC, 1990a).

3   Unless otherwise noted, the texts of the BITs mentioned in this study may be found in the United Nations Treaty Series and in the collection of BITs maintained by the International Centre for Settlement of Investment Disputes (ICSID) (ICSID, 1972-).

4   Unless otherwise noted, all instruments cited herein may be found in UNCTAD, 1996.

Section II

STOCKTAKING AND ANALYSIS

As noted in section I, in treaty practice the national treatment standard has been widely used in trade agreements. More recently, the standard has been extended to the sphere of FDI through its adoption in bilateral, regional, plurilateral and multilateral investment-related instruments. It has also been reflected in national laws. Developed countries generally include the principle of national treatment in their constitutions or basic laws (UNCTAD, 1994, p. 303). Equally, according to a World Bank survey of some 51 investment codes adopted by developing countries, the overwhelming majority of these countries have adopted provisions that aim at avoiding differences in treatment between foreign and local investors. Many of those countries have favoured a definition of national treatment which excludes the possibility of granting more favourable treatment to FDI, through the use of a test of treatment similar or equal to that given to local investors (World Bank, 1992).

Existing IIAs have taken at least three major policy approaches towards national treatment, which are discussed next.

A. An agreement does not mention national treatment

Some agreements that otherwise provide standards of treatment for foreign investors do not grant national treatment. This (unusual) approach is exemplified by the Assocation of South-East Asian Nations (ASEAN) Agreement for the Protection and Promotion of Investments and the early BITs signed by China, Norway and Sweden. Article 2 of China's BIT with Sweden spells out the general standards of treatment granted to foreign investors as follows:

"(1) Each Contracting State shall at all times ensure fair and equitable treatment to the investments by investors of the other Contracting State.

(2) Investments by investors of either Contracting State in the territory of the other Contracting State shall not be subjected to a treatment less favourable than that accorded to investments by investors of third States.

(3) Notwithstanding the provisions of paragraph (2) of this Article, a Contracting State, which has concluded with one or more other States an agreement regarding the formation of a customs union or free-trade area, shall be free to grant a more favourable treatment to investments by investors of the State or States, which are also parties to the said agreement, or by investors of some of these States. A Contracting State shall also be free to grant a more favourable treatment to investments by investors of other States, if this is stipulated under bilateral agreements concluded with such States before the date of the signature of this Agreement."

The omission of the national treatment standard may be explained in certain cases on the ground that the host country does not wish to extend preferential treatment enjoyed by its domestic enterprises to foreign enterprises. On the other hand, the reasons for not including the standard may be very specific to the situation in question. In some cases, for example, granting national treatment has been complicated by the provision of price subsidies for national State enterprises for utilities such as water and electricity. In situations where many firms remain State-owned it is difficult to grant the same price subsidies to foreign investors (and perhaps also to national private investors). Finally, home countries might not have found it worthwhile to insist on the granting of national treatment standard in host countries where the conditions available to national firms were below a certain minimum. Over the years China has changed its policy towards national treatment and has agreed to grant it in certain treaties.[1]

C. An agreement contains a general national treatment clause

At the outset, it should be pointed out that national treatment provisions follow a standard general pattern. However, considerable scope for variation arises in the context of that pattern, each variant having significant implications for the process of economic development.

The first question that arises is whether it is the investment, the investor or both that are to receive national treatment. National treatment clauses typically address this question although their approaches vary considerably. In some BITs it is the investment that is entitled to national treatment. Others refer to "enterprises and the activities of enterprises".[2] These formulations would seem to exclude "investors" in the enterprise from national treatment in such matters as, for example, taxation. To guard against such results, an increasing number of IIAs include separate provisions granting the investor and the investment national treatment. Examples of this approach include the the BIT between Jamaica and the United Kingdom (article 3), NAFTA (article 1102 (1) and (2)) and the Asian-African Legal Consultative Committee (AALCC) model BITs A and B (article 5 Draft A and B, UNCTAD, 1996, vol. III, pp. 119, 130).[3] In some contexts, on the other hand, the term "investment" could be interpreted as covering "investors" because of the inextricable linkage between the investment and the investor.

1. Scope of application

a. *Extent of coverage of the investment process*

As noted in section I, a national treatment clause can apply either to the pre- and post-entry stage or to the post entry stage only. The post-entry model is at present much more common. However, some recent IIAs have extended national treatment to the pre-entry stage through a combined pre- and post-entry clause. Finally, the operation of national treatment in the General Agreement on Trade in Services (GATS) offers a unique hybrid approach which requires separate consideration.

B. An agreement goes beyond a general national treat clause and involves a more specific non-discrimination re

Here national treatment is present in the content of subst rules rather than in any single statement of the standard. I be a fundamental part of the legal order created by the re The legal order of the European Union is the main exam| this approach. National treatment plays a significant role Community legal order, particularly as regards entry and establish (UNCTAD, 1999c, pp. 22-23). In addition, European Unio applies a wider concept of non-discrimination between nat of member States to specific policy areas, thereby helping to harm national standards and to develop an integrated single m for trade and investment (box 1).

Box 1. Measures adopted by the European Union aimed at abolishing discrimination between nationals of different member States [a]

- general prohibition against discrimination on the groun nationality (article 12);
- free movement of goods (articles 28-29);
- state monopolies (article 31);
- free movement of workers (article 39 (2));
- entry and establishment (articles 43-48);
- freedom to provide services (articles 49-55);
- free movement of capital (articles 56-60);
- social security (Regulation 1408/71 article 3(1));
- competition (article 81(1) (d), 82 (c));
- state aids (articles 87-88);
- discriminatory taxation (articles 90-91).

[a] References are to the Treaty of Rome as amended by the Treaty of Ams (which entered into force on 1 May 1999) (EU, 1997), unless otherwise

---

(i)   The post-entry model

This model is typified by IIAs that restrict the operation of the treaty to investments from other contracting parties that are admitted in accordance with the laws and regulations of the host contracting party (UNCTAD, 1999c, pp. 17-20). This is followed with a provision that accords national treatment to investments so admitted. For example, the BIT between Germany and Namibia stipulates in article 2 that each contracting party shall promote as far as possible investments by nationals or companies of the other contracting party and "admit such investments in accordance with its legislation". Then, in article 3, the national treatment standard is introduced. This provision is divided into four paragraphs. Article 3 (1) states:

> "Neither Contracting Party shall subject investments in its territory owned or controlled by nationals or companies of the other Contracting Party to treatment less favourable than it accords to investments of its own nationals or companies or to investments of nationals or companies of any third State."

Article 3 (2) repeats the same basic phraseology but substitutes "investments" with a reference to "nationals or companies of the other Contracting Party" and accords to them national treatment "as regards their activity in connection with investments in its territory". This approach is followed closely in other BITs signed by European countries.[4]

The National Treatment Decision contained in the OECD Declaration on International Investment and Multinational Enterprises of 1976 makes clear in paragraph II (4) that "this Declaration does not deal with the right of Member countries to regulate the entry of foreign investment or the conditions of establishment of foreign enterprises" (UNCTAD, 1996, vol. II, p. 184). Under the OECD regime, matters of entry and establishment are the concern of the OECD Code of Liberalisation of Capital Movements in which the right of establishment was introduced in 1984 (UNCTAD, 1999c,

p. 24). Taken together, the Code of Liberalisation of Capital Movements and the National Treatment instrument cover both pre- and post-entry treatment of investment. In order to ensure consistency between these two instruments, the Committee on Capital Movements and Invisible Transactions, the body responsible for the administration of the Codes, and the Committee on International Investment and Multinational Enterprises, the body responsible for the administration and review of the Declaration, cooperate over the interrelationship between the two instruments. According to the 1991 review of the Declaration, measures affecting investment by "direct branches" (branches whose parent company is a non-resident) are covered by the Capital Movements Code, while those of "indirect branches" (branches whose parent company is an established subsidiary of a non-resident) continue to be covered by the National Treatment instrument (OECD, 1992, p. 34). It should be noted that the OECD National Treatment instrument contains no legal obligation, but it is subject to a legally binding system of notification and examination of member countries' exceptions to national treatment. (This is briefly described below under the subheading on exceptions.) In sum, the OECD approach to national treatment has evolved over the years from its original post-entry model to a system that covers both entry and post-entry activities.

Other instruments that have followed the post-entry national treatment model include:

*   Many BITs signed between developing countries.[5]

*   The Energy Charter Treaty, article 10 (7), extends national treatment to the operations of foreign investments/investors after they enter the host country:

    "Each Contracting Party shall accord to Investments in its Area of Investors of other Contracting Parties, and their related activities including management, maintenance, use, enjoyment or disposal, treatment no less favourable than that which it accords to

Investments of its own Investors or of the Investors of any other Contracting Party or any third state and their related activities including management, maintenance, use, enjoyment or disposal, whichever is the most favourable" (UNCTAD, 1996, vol. II, p. 556).

As regards the making of investments, contracting parties are only required to "endeavour to accord" national treatment. But the Agreement provides for subsequent negotiation and conclusion of a "supplementary treaty" that will "oblige" parties to accord national and MFN treatment (article 10 (2)-(4), UNCTAD, 1996, p. 555). The negotiations have been concluded, but the Charter Conference has not yet adopted the text (UNCTAD, 1999c, p. 42).

• In the framework of MERCOSUR, investments of investors from non-member States, in contrast to investments of investors from member States, do not enjoy pre-entry national treatment. They are entitled to national treatment only after entry (Decision 11/94, UNCTAD, 1996, vol.II, p. 530).

(ii)   The pre- and post-entry model

The pre- and post-entry approach has its origins in United States treaty practice. Clauses to this effect were present in United States FCN treaties, and have been continued in the BITs signed by the United States and, more recently, by Canada. The United States model BIT (1994) states, in article II (1):

"With respect to the establishment, acquisition, expansion, management, conduct, operation and sale or other disposition of covered investments, each Party shall accord treatment no less favorable than that it accords, in like situations, to investments in its territory of its own nationals or companies (hereinafter "national treatment") or to investments in its territory of nationals or companies of a third country (hereinafter "most favored nation treatment"),

> whichever is most favorable (hereinafter "national and most favored nation treatment") ..." (UNCTAD, 1996, vol. III, p. 197).

This provision makes entry to the host State subject to the national (and MFN) treatment standard in addition to post-entry treatment. This general commitment is typically made subject to the right of each party to adopt or maintain exceptions falling within one of the sectors or matters listed in the annex to the BIT (United States model BIT, 1994, article II (2)).[6]

At the regional level -- apart from the OECD instruments and the ECT (which appears to represent a transition from post- to pre-establishment coverage) -- a significant example of the pre- and post-entry national treatment model is the NAFTA.[7] Article 1102 of the NAFTA grants national treatment to investors and investments of another contracting party with respect to "the establishment, acquisition, expansion, management, conduct, operation, and sale or other disposition of investments" (UNCTAD, 1996, vol. III, p. 74).

Other agreements follow a similar approach:

- The Asia Pacific Economic Cooperation (APEC) Non-Binding Investment Principles extend the national treatment standard to "the establishment, expansion, operation and protection..." of investments by foreign investors (UNCTAD, 1996, vol.II, p. 536). However, the APEC instrument is non-binding and represents only a "best efforts" commitment.

- The 1994 Treaty on Free Trade between Colombia, Mexico and Venezuela (article 17-03) accords national treatment (and MFN) to investors of another party and their investments (subject *inter alia* to the right of each party to impose special formalities in connection with the establishment of an investment and to impose information requirements) (http:www.sice.oas.org/Trade/G3_E/G3E_TOC.stm).

• In MERCOSUR, investments of investors from other MERCOSUR member States are to be admitted on the basis of treatment no less favourable than that accorded to domestic investors or investors from third States, subject to the right of each member State to maintain exceptional limitations for a transitional period, which must be detailed in an annex to the Protocol (Decision 11/93 of the Council of MERCOSUR of 17 January 1994, in UNCTAD, 1996, vol.II. pp. 513 and 520 for listed exceptions).

• The Framework Agreement on the ASEAN Investment Area adopted in 1998 accords national treatment "immediately to ASEAN investors and their investments, in respect of all industries and measures affecting investment including but not limited to the admission, establishment, acquisition, expansion, management, operation and disposition of investments" (article 7.1 (b)), subject to exceptions provided for under the Agreement (see below). Furthermore, article 4 states that the ASEAN Investment Area will be an area where "national treatment is extended to ASEAN investors by 2010, and to all investors by 2020" (article 4 (b)).[8]

As noted, the pre- and post-entry approach is not as widespread in terms of numbers of investment agreements as the post-entry model. This approach was followed in the draft text of the Multilateral Agreement on Investment (MAI) (OECD, 1998b, p. 13). Apart from the United States BITs, the other examples deal not only with investment but also with wider trading arrangements.

(iii) The GATS hybrid model

The GATS is based on the principle of "progressive liberalization". Accordingly, the obligation of national treatment expressed in article XVII of the GATS is not a general obligation applicable to trade in servies in all sectors and by all members, but a specific commitment that applies only in sectors inscribed in a member's schedule, and its application is to be gradually extended to other sectors through successive rounds of negotiations. Furthermore, if a member decides to include a sector in its schedule, it still retains the possibility of deciding the level of national treatment it proposes to grant in that sector by listing specific limitations it wishes to maintain. Those limitations could actually be specific discriminatory measures that are inconsistent with the national treatment standard. However, by scheduling them, a member would maintain the legal right to continue to apply them.

The national treatment obligation in article XVII of the GATS requires each member to extend to services and service suppliers of other members treatment no less favourable than that it extends to like services and service suppliers of national origin.[9] Paragraph 1 of that article states:

"1.   In sectors inscribed in its Schedule, and subject to any conditions and qualifications set out therein, each Member shall accord to services and service suppliers of any other Member, in respect of all measures affecting the supply of services, treatment no less favourable than that it accords to its own like services and service suppliers."

This may be achieved by according formally identical or formally different treatment. In other words, a national treatment commitment under the GATS would prohibit any form of discrimination whether *de jure* or *de facto*. Paragraphs 2 and 3 of article XVII state:

"2.   A Member may meet the requirement of paragraph 1 by according to services and service suppliers of any other Member, either formally identical treatment or formally different treatment to that it accords to its own like services and service suppliers.

3.   Formally identical or formally different treatment shall be considered to be less favourable if it modifies the conditions of competition in favour of services or service suppliers of the Member compared to like services or service suppliers of any other Member."

This is meant to ensure that the national treatment obligation provides foreign service suppliers with equal opportunities to compete in a domestic market. This provision is quite far-reaching in the sense that it would cover anything that "modifies conditions of competition" in favour of foreign service suppliers (who under mode 3 would be foreign investors).

As stated earlier, the national treatment obligation of the GATS applies to "all measures affecting the supply of services". Moreover, measures by members are defined in article 1 of the GATS as measures taken by central, regional or local governments and authorities and by non-governmental bodies in the exercise of powers delegated by all government authorities. According to article XVII of the GATS, furthermore, national treatment is to be granted to service suppliers as well as services of any other member.

b. The meaning of national treatment in relation to subnational authorities

It is clear that national treatment obligations apply to the host country Government and governmental bodies. Also, as a matter of the law of treaties, a treaty applies to the entire territory of a party unless a different intention appears from the treaty or is otherwise established. However, it is not always so clear in practice what national treatment means in relation to the political subdivisions of a State. This problem (which is also relevant to other clauses in IIAs) can become significant where a subnational authority has a constitutional power to make investment policy. Such power may be used to grant preferential treatment to local, as opposed to out-of-sub-division investors, as, for example, where a host subnational authority is seeking to encourage the growth of local small and medium-sized firms. A question that arises is whether a subnational authority has to extend such preferential treatment to foreign inward investors on the basis of the national treatment standard, regardless of how it treats national investors from outside the sub-division.

The question has been answered in the provisions of some IIAs, such as United States BITs which, following the United States model BIT (article XV) (UNCTAD, 1996, vol. III, p. 204) state that the obligations of the treaty will apply to the political sub-divisions of the parties.[10] The United States model BIT specifies further that, in the case of a United States state, territory or possession national treatment means "treatment no less favorable than the treatment accorded thereby, in like situations, to investments from nationals of the United States of America resident in, and companies legally constituted under the laws and regulations of, other States, Territories or possessions of the United States of America" (article XV, (1) (b)). According to this provision, it appears that a foreign investor is to be treated by a United States subnational authority as if it were an investor from another United States subnational authority for the purpose of compliance with national treatment disciplines. Thus, if the host subnational state offers preferential treatment to local investors and does not extend such treatment to out-of-state investors, the foreign investor cannot invoke national treatment to obtain similar preferences. All that the foreign investor can do is require treatment no less favourable than that accorded to out-of-state United States investors. Although the United States model is ambiguous on the issue, it may be presumed that the comparable treatment should be with the best treated out-of-state United States investor, otherwise the treatment would be "less favourable".

This issue is made clearer in NAFTA article 1102 (3) which states that the treatment involved should be "no less favorable than the most favourable treatment accorded, in like circumstances, by that state or province to investors, and to investments of investors, of the Party of which it forms a part." This formulation can allow for differential treatment as between different out-of-sub-division investors of the host country. What it would not allow, however, is for the foreign investor to receive the worst treatment offered to out-of-sub-division investors. In the light of the words, "the most favourable treatment accorded" the foreign investor must be given the best available treatment offered to such local investors.[11]

The OECD National Treatment instrument specifically refers to the problem of subnational entities. By paragraph 3 thereof, "Member countries will endeavour to ensure that their territorial sub-divisions apply national treatment". This provision applies to "states, provinces, cantons, municipalities, regions and communities, but not to national government lands, and it covers areas of legislation in which powers of states are not subordinated to those of the national government" (OECD, 1993, pp. 26-27). The phrasing of the provision suggests that in some cases a member Government may not be in a position to "ensure" that territorial subdivisions apply national treatment. The OECD applies the following criteria to determine whether the treatment of a foreign investor by a territorial sub-division constitutes an exception to national treatment that must be notified to the OECD (OECD, 1993, p. 27):

- An exception exists where all domestic enterprises, both in-state and out-of-state, are given the same treatment, and the foreign investor is given less favourable treatment than these domestic enterprises.

- Where there are differences in the treatment of in-state and out-of-state domestic enterprises, differential treatment of out-of-state foreign-controlled enterprises by the territorial subdivision in question need not, in itself, constitute an exception to national treatment. In such cases the measures in question should be examined pragmatically, taking into account the extent to which the foreign-controlled and domestic enterprises concerned are placed in the same circumstances. Such measures are to be reported to the OECD in the interests of transparency.

- In determining whether a measure constitutes an exception, it is important to identify whether the discrimination implied by a measure is actually motivated, at least in part, by the fact that the enterprises affected are under foreign control. Here difficulties as to what is "foreign" may be encountered as enterprises from outside the territorial sub-division, both domestic and foreign-controlled, may be treated as "foreign" to that jurisdiction.

Turning to non-governmental associations or regulatory bodies, the OECD National Treatment instrument covers, in principle, measures of regulatory bodies only if they are attributable to

Governments. However, there is an exception with regard to banking and finance. Here, all associations and regulatory bodies are covered, whether or not there is government involvement. In a similar vein, the MAI negotiating text made membership of self-regulatory bodies and associations in the field of financial services subject to national treatment (OECD, 1998b, p. 83).

2. The substantive content of the national treatment standard

The substantive content of the national treatment standard involves, in particular, an analysis of the following two issues: the factual situation in which the standard applies and the definition of the standard itself.

a. *Factual situations in which national treatment applies*

Some IIAs qualify the definition of the national treatment standard by specifying the factual situations in which the standard applies. The following alternatives present themselves:

(i) The "same" or "identical" circumstances

The most restrictive formulation would be to limit national treatment to the "same" or "identical" circumstances. This would offer a narrow scope to national treatment as the incidence of an "identical" situation may be hard to show. Such a formulation was proposed during the drafting of article 49 of the 1983 text of the United Nations Draft Code of Conduct on Transnational Corporations (UNCTC, 1990b, p. 200).

Earlier BITs signed by the United Kingdom referred to the "same circumstances". For example, the 1982 BIT between Belize and the United Kingdom, article 3 (1), provides that "Neither Contracting Party shall... subject investments or returns of nationals or companies of the other Contracting Party to treatment less favourable than that which it accords in the same circumstances to investments or returns of its own nationals" (Dolzer and Stevens, 1995, p. 63). The more recent practice of the United Kingdom is not to qualify the national treatment standard.

(ii)   The economic activities and/or industries to which national treatment applies

Some IIAs specify the economic activities or industries to which national treatment applies. Such an approach has the effect of narrowing the scope of national treatment to those areas of activity expressly mentioned in the agreement (box 2). It is another example of an approach which is used by host countries to preserve a degree of flexibility to act by narrowing the scope of national treatment. This is also the effect sought by the GATS provisions already mentioned above. National treatment is expected to apply only to those sectors to which commitments have been made.

Such functional delineation of national treatment can also arise as a result of the specialized nature of an agreement. (See also section III, interactions between the scope and definitions and the national treatment provisions.) This is the case in, for example, the GATS which limits its functional scope to services, thought this is in itself a vast area of commercial activity. Other agreements in which the functional scope of national treatment is similarly circumscribed include, in relation to the energy industries, the Energy Charter Treaty; in relation to intellectual property rights, the TRIPS Agreement (article 3); and, in relation to specific operational measures, the TRIMs Agreement. Some specialized agreements further specify their functional delineation in the formulation of the national treatment clause. Thus, for example, under article XVII, GATS specifies that "each Member shall accord to *services and service suppliers* of any other Member, in respect of *all measures affecting the supply of services*, treatment no less favourable than that it accords to its own like *services and service suppliers*" (emphasis added).[12]

The ILO Tripartite Declaration of Principles Concerning Multinational Enterprises and Social Policy uses a standard similar to that of national treatment where it provides that wages, benefits and conditions of work and standards of industrial relations to be observed by TNCs should be not less favourable than those observed by comparable employers in the country concerned (UNCTAD, 1996, vol. I, pp. 96-97). However, it must be made clear that the ILO Declaration uses a comparison between standards observed by TNCs and comparable domestic employers to determine the minimum obligations of TNCs. Thus, it could be said that where TNCs observe only the same standards as domestic employers, and these fall below the minimum standards required by the ILO Declaration, TNCs should observe the higher standards of the Declaration.

Box 2. Examples of functional delineations of national treatment

Agreements delineating the functional scope of national treatment include:

The *Common Convention on Investments in the States of the Customs and Economic Union of Central Africa*, article 3, offers a functional list of cases to which the same conditions should apply as between undertakings whose capital derives from other countries and undertakings in the member countries of the Union (UNCTAD, 1996, vol. II, p. 89).

The *Agreement for the Establishment of a Regime for CARICOM Enterprises* (of 1987), article 12 (4), extends national treatment for CARICOM enterprises to specific functions comprising licences and permissions necessary for the proper conduct of affairs, the purchase or use of goods and services, access to credit, and protection by quantitative restrictions or other forms of protection against imports from third countries (UNCTAD, 1996, vol. II, p. 277).

The BIT between Denmark and Indonesia (article 3) refers not to "treatment" but to the "imposition of conditions". This language suggests that the host country is not obliged to give national treatment with respect to benefits and advantages.

Decision 292 of the Commission of the Cartagena Agreement, article 9, offers national treatment for Andean multinational enterprises with respect to preferences and for the acquisition of public sector goods and services (UNCTAD, 1996, vol. II, p. 477).

Another approach that has been used is to have an open-ended but indicative list of activities to which the national treatment standard applies (box 3). For example, the Energy Charter Treaty, article 10 (7), specifies that national treatment applies to investments of investors of other contracting parties and "their related activities, including management, maintenance, use, enjoyment or disposal..." (UNCTAD, 1996, vol. II, p. 556). Thus, while it is an agreement aimed at the energy sector only, this formulation makes it clear that it encompasses all types of activities associated with the operation of an energy investment.[13]

Box 3. Examples of national treatment clauses covering a broad range of investment activities

The *World Bank Guidelines on the Treatment of Foreign Direct Investment* (1992) offer a functional list of areas to which national treatment applies. Thus, Guideline III (3) (a) states:

"With respect to the protection and security of their person, property rights and interests, and to the granting of permits, import and export licenses and the authorization to employ, and the issuance of the necessary entry and stay visas to their foreign personnel and other legal matters relevant to the treatment of foreign investors.....such treatment will, subject to the requirement of fair and equitable treatment mentioned above, be as favourable as that accorded by the State to national investors in similar circumstances..." (UNCTAD, 1996, vol. I, pp. 249-250).

NAFTA article 1102 (1) lists "the establishment, acquisition, expansion, management, conduct, operation and sale or other disposition of investments.." as being subject to national treatment (UNCTAD, 1996, vol. III, p. 74).

The *draft MAI* uses the following formulation: "establishment, acquisition, expansion, operation, management, maintenance, use, enjoyment and sale or other disposition of investments" (OECD, 1998b, p. 13). This formulation was considered by several delegations to be a

/...

Box 3 (concluded)

comprehensive one whose terms were intended to cover all activities of investors and their investments for both the pre- and post-establishment phases. Other delegations favoured a closed list of investment activities covered by national treatment. Others objected to this approach on the grounds that, while such a list had the advantage of certainty, it could omit elements that were of importance to the investor (OECD, 1998a, p. 11).

The *Framework Agreement on the ASEAN Investment Area*, as noted above, offers an interesting variant of this approach. By article 7 (1) (b), national treatment is accorded immediately to ASEAN investors and their investments in respect of all industries and measures affecting investment, "including but not limited to the admission, establishment, acquisition, expansion, management, operation and disposition of investments" (ASEAN, 1998). This approach makes clear that the list is only illustrative and not exhaustive as to cases in which national treatment applies.

Listing specific activities to which national treatment applies -- even if the lists are only indicative and not closed lists -- serve the purpose of providing guidance as to which types of activities the parties intended to cover under a national treatment provision and which were not to be so covered. Given the potentially broad range of activities to which national treatment may apply, such lists, whose coverage may vary considerably from instrument to instrument (box 3), respond to a concern that, otherwise, open-ended national treatment clauses (or national treatment clauses that are silent about the types of activities covered) may result in extending national treatment to aspects that were never intended by the parties.

It may be asked whether such wide wording results in "overkill" in that it may be difficult in practice to see the difference between words such as "management", "use", "enjoyment" or "maintenance".

(iii) "Like situations", "similar situations" or "like circumstances"

Qualifications such as "like situations", "similar situations" and "like circumstances" may be seen as synonymous and therefore can be discussed together. They may be less restrictive of national treatment in that they may apply to any activity or sector that is not subject to exceptions. What is a "like" situation or circumstance is a matter that needs to be determined in the light of the facts of the case. This assumes that clear comparisons of business situations are possible, and that agreement can be reached on what is a "like" circumstance. This may not be easy in practice, as the experience of GATT/WTO Dispute Panels has shown (Mattoo, 1997). It is implicit in the use of this term that the host country will assess cases in good faith and in full consideration of all relevant facts. According to an OECD report, among the most important matters to be considered are "whether the two enterprises are in the same sector; the impact of policy objectives of the host country in particular fields; and the motivation behind the measure involved" (OECD, 1985, pp. 16-17). A key issue in such cases is to "ascertain whether the discrimination is motivated, at least in part, by the fact that the enterprises concerned are under foreign control" (OECD, 1993, p. 22).

The "like situations" formulation is found in, for example, United States BITs, following the United States model BIT (article II (1), UNCTAD, 1996, vol. III, p. 197) and in the OECD National Treatment instrument (UNCTAD, 1996, vol. II, p. 184). The "like circumstances" formulation is found in NAFTA (article 1102 (1), (2), UNCTAD, 1996, vol. III, p. 74) and in the Canada-Chile Free Trade Agreement (article G-02 (1) (2), Canada-Chile, 1997). The World Bank Guidelines on the Treatment of Foreign Investment use "in similar circumstances" (UNCTAD, 1996, vol. I, p. 250). These are general phrases which allow considerable scope for determining what is "like" from the context surrounding an investor and an investment.

A variation of this approach is found in the Framework Agreement on the ASEAN Investment Area, which, after listing the functions to which national treatment applies, specifies that the treatment concerned will be that which the host country accords "to its own like investors and investments" (article 7 (1) (b), ASEAN, 1998). Here the comparison shifts from the general context of the investment to the nature and characteristics of investors and investments, a more exacting comparison.

The inclusion of the phrase "in like circumstances" was debated during the MAI negotiations, and no agreement was reached on its inclusion. Some delegations thought that national treatment implicitly provides the comparative context for determining whether a measure unduly treats foreign investments differently and that the inclusion of the words was unnecessary and open to abuse. Other delegations thought that the comparative context should be indicated, following the practice of the OECD National Treatment instrument, NAFTA and some BITs (OECD, 1998a, p. 11).[14]

(iv) No factual comparisons

A significant number of IIAs contain a description of the national treatment standard but are silent on whether national treatment applies to specified activities or like situations or circumstances. Here a simple reference is made to investors and/ or investments, usually in separate paragraphs, followed by a description of the standard of treatment required. Such an approach is seen in, for example, the Chilean, French, German, Swiss and United Kingdom model BITs, though the last retains a functional delimitation formula in relation to the treatment of investors. This approach offers the widest scope for comparison as, in principle, any matter that is relevant to determining whether the foreign investor is being given national treatment can be considered. The test will be an easier one for the investor than under formulations requiring proof of like situations, circumstances and/or functional contexts.

b. Definition of the standard

IIAs have defined the standard of national treatment in two main ways. One way requires a strict standard of equality of treatment between national and foreign investors. The other offers the possibility of granting more favourable treatment to foreign investors.

(i)   "Same" or "as favourable as" treatment[15]

This formulation suggests that the treatment offered to foreign investors is no better than that received by national investors. In effect it excludes the possibility of the foreign investor claiming preferential treatment as a matter of treaty obligation on the part of the host country. However, there is nothing in this formulation to prevent a host country from treating foreign investors in a preferential way, should it so choose. National investors may challenge such preferential treatment. They may have rights under the host country law to challenge such treatment, for example, under national constitutional provisions against discrimination. In addition, the IIA might itself be incorporated into national law. This may have the effect of extending protection to national investors as well, although much depends on the actual wording of the agreement and the extent to which national laws give rights to domestic investors in such cases.

Examples of such an approach include:

• The Agreement on Investment and Free Movement of Arab Capital Among Arab Countries states in article 4 that "[m]ember states undertake to treat Arab investments in all areas designated thereto, without discrimination and on equal footing with indigenous investments" (UNCTAD, 1996, vol. II, p. 122). The Unified Agreement for the Investment of Arab Capital in the Arab States requires that "the capital of the Arab investor shall, without discrimination, be treated in the same manner as capital owned by the citizens of that State" (article 6, UNCTAD, 1996, vol. II, p. 214).[16]

• The Common Convention on Investments in the States of the Customs and Economic Union of Central Africa, article 3, states that "[u]ndertakings whose capital derives from other countries, shall be able to acquire rights of any kind deemed necessary for the exercise of their activities: real property and industrial rights, concessions, official authorisations and permits, participations in government contracts under the same conditions as undertakings in the member countries of the Union" (UNCTAD, 1996, vol. II, p. 89).

*   The Joint Convention on the Freedom of Movement of Persons and the Right of Establishment in the Central African Customs and Economic Union (CACEU), article 3, provides that, "Nationals of CACEU member States travelling, staying or establishing themselves in the territory of another member State shall enjoy the same rights and freedoms as the nationals thereof, except for political rights, " which are defined as "(a) the individual rights and guarantees; (b) the personal and public freedoms" (UNCTAD, 1996, vol. II, p. 156).

*   The Community Investment Code of the Economic Community of the Great Lakes Countries (article 9) also uses a reference to the "same conditions as enterprises of the host country" (UNCTAD, 1996, vol. II, p. 255).

*   Decision 291of the Commission of the Cartagena Agreement (ANCOM) (1991) article 2, provides that "Foreign investors shall have the same rights and obligations as national investors, except as otherwise provided in the legislation of each member country" (UNCTAD, 1996, vol. II, p. 450). Decision 24, which preceded Decision 291, was more blunt: "Member countries may not accord to foreign investors treatment more favourable than to national investors." Thus the ANCOM position has shifted from an outright prohibition of preferential treatment for foreign investors to one of leaving to member countries the discretion whether or not to accord to those investors the same, less favourable or more favourable treatment than to national investors.

*   The World Bank Guidelines on the Treatment of Foreign Direct Investment require treatment that is "as favourable as that accorded by the State to national investors in similar circumstances"(UNCTAD, 1996, vol. I, p. 250).

*   The draft United Nations Code of Conduct on Transnational Corporations, in its 1983 version, included two alternative formulations in brackets. The first one was "the treatment"

and the second formulation was "treatment no less favourable" than that accorded to domestic enterprises (UNCTAD, 1996, vol. I, p. 173).

(ii)   "No less favourable" treatment

This formulation, which is the most commonly used in IIAs, offers treatment which will usually result in treatment as favourable as that received by national investors of a host country. However, it leaves open the possibility of subjecting host country actions to review in accordance with standards of treatment that may be in practice more favourable for foreign, as compared to national, investors. This may occur where standards of treatment accorded to national investors who are in situations comparable to those of foreign investors fall below international minimum standards. Again any consequential discrimination suffered by national investors would be beyond the scope of an IIA, though it may be subject to the same remedies under national law for national investors as mentioned in relation to the issue of "same" or "as favourable as" treatment, with the rider that the possibility of more favourable treatment for foreign investors is implied in the "no less favourable" formulation.

The principal example of this approach is the OECD National Treatment instrument contained in the OECD Declaration on International Investment and Multinational Enterprises of 1976 (UNCTAD, 1996, vol. II, p. 184; Muchlinski, 1995, pp. 583-587). According to the Declaration:

".. Member countries should, consistent with their needs to maintain public order, to protect their essential security interests and to fulfil commitments relating to international peace and security, accord to enterprises operating in their territories and owned or controlled directly or indirectly by nationals of another Member country (hereinafter referred to as "Foreign-Controlled Enterprises") treatment under their laws, regulations and administrative practices, consistent with international law and no less

favourable than that accorded in like situations to
domestic enterprises (hereinafter referred to as
"National Treatment")."

The meaning and effect of the OECD National Treatment instrument
has been regularly reviewed by the Committee on International
Investment and Multinational Enterprises under powers granted
to it by article 4 (a) of the Third Revised Council Decision on
National Treatment (OECD, 1994). This has resulted in the Committee
issuing guidelines for the interpretation of the principle as described
in the Declaration (OECD, 1985, 1992, 1993). Furthermore, as
part of its monitoring functions, the Committee has undertaken
periodic surveys of member country measures that constitute
exceptions to the "national treatment" principle, based upon its
clarifications of the 1976 Declaration.

Thus, in OECD practice, according to the Committee's reports
on national treatment, the phrase in the Declaration "treatment
no less favourable than that accorded to domestic enterprises"
has the following implications (OECD, 1985, 1993):

• An exception to national treatment is not created by the
existence of a public monopoly which results in discriminatory
measures against foreign affiliates.

• If a foreign affiliate already established in a member country
receives less favourable treatment, this can constitute an
exception to national treatment if it also falls within the other
criteria for determining such an exception; on the other
hand, if the foreign affiliate receives treatment at least as
favourable as that given to domestic enterprises, there can
be no case of an exception to national treatment.

• In cases where domestic enterprises do not all receive the
same treatment, where a foreign affiliate already established
in a member country is treated less favourably than the least
well treated domestic enterprise, this can constitute an
exception to national treatment; if it receives treatment
equivalent to that given to the best treated domestic enterprise

there can be no question of an exception to national treatment. In cases where a foreign affiliate receives treatment at least as favourable as the least well treated domestic enterprise but less favourable than the best treated enterprise, it is not certain that this constitutes an exception to national treatment.

- Each such case should be reviewed on its facts, taking account of individual national characteristics and the degree to which the foreign and domestic enterprises are placed in comparable circumstances.

- The reference to international law ensures that international minimum standards of treatment for aliens and their property, recognized by the member countries of the OECD, form part of the substantive test of treatment. This allows for the preferential treatment of foreign investors where national treatment falls below such international standards.

The "no less favourable treatment" standard is the most common formulation in treaty practice. It was also included in the MAI negotiating text (OECD, 1998b, p. 13). There was discussion as to whether the "same" or "comparable" treatment should be used, but the majority of delegates considered that this would unacceptably weaken the standard of treatment from the investor's viewpoint (OECD, 1998a, p. 10). Other agreements that use the "no less favourable treatment" formulation are listed in box 4.

Box 4. Other agreements using the "no less favourable" formulation

- The AALCC draft model BITs, article 5, models A and B; Chilean model BIT, article 4 (2); French model BIT, article 4; German model BIT, article 3 (1) (2); Dutch model BIT, article 3(2) (Netherlands, 1997); Portuguese model BIT, article 3 (2); Swiss model BIT, article 4 (2) (3); United Kingdom model BIT, article 3 (1) (2); United States model BIT, article II (1), and the majority of BITs that follow these models.

- NAFTA, article 1102; Canada-Chile Free Trade Agreement, article G-02 (Canada-Chile, 1997).

/...

Box 4 (concluded)

- CARICOM Agreement for the Establishment of a Regime for CARICOM Enterprises, article 12 (4) (a) (b) (c) (g).
- MERCOSUR Decision 11/93, article 3 (Protocol on Intrazonal Investors), and Decision 11/94 Section C (2) (Protocol on Extrazonal Investors).
- Energy Charter Treaty, article 10 (7).
- Framework Agreement on the ASEAN Investment Area, article 7 (1) (b) (ASEAN, 1998).
- GATS, article XVII (1); TRIPS Agreement, article 3 (1).

---

3. *"De jure"* and *"de facto"* national treatment

As noted in section I, national treatment is primarily concerned with provisions in the national laws and regulations of host countries which specifically address the treatment of foreign investors. However, foreign investors may find themselves in disadvantageous situations vis-à-vis local investors as a result of regulations or practices that, although not discriminatory against them *per se*, nevertheless have a detrimental effect on their ability to operate in practice, precisely because of their being "foreign". A few IIAs have explicitly addressed this issue. An example of a provision that expressly deals with *de facto* as well as *de jure* treatment is article XVII of the GATS which states, in paragraphs 2 and 3:

> " 2. A Member may meet the requirement of paragraph 1 by according to services and service suppliers of any other Member, either formally identical treatment or formally different treatment to that it accords to its own like services and service providers.
>
> 3. Formally identical or formally different treatment shall be considered to be less favourable if it modifies the conditions of competition in favour of services

---

or service suppliers of the Member compared to like services or service suppliers of any other Member." (UNCTAD, 1996, vol. I, p. 302).

These provisions are of special significance in relation to financial services or insurance, where it is often the case that identical treatment cannot be granted to branches and other unincorporated entities of foreign controlled enterprises in view of the need to maintain prudential measures or because of legal/technical differences. In such cases, differences of treatment between domestic and foreign controlled enterprises may be justifiable provided that the difference in treatment is no greater than strictly necessary to meet prudential requirements and that *de facto* the competitive opportunities on the market for foreign investors are not unfavourably affected. This approach is often referred to as "equivalent treatment" (OECD, 1993, pp. 22-23).

4. "Stand alone" national treatment provision or national treatment combined with other general standards of treatment

The standard of national treatment is often combined in IIAs with other standards of treatment. The basic alternatives are described below.

a. *"Stand alone" national treatment provision*

In certain cases national treatment is the only general standard of treatment that an instrument seeks to grant. The OECD National Treatment instrument focuses on this standard and requires that member countries "consider applying 'National Treatment' in respect of countries other than Member countries" (paragraph 2, UNCTAD, 1996, vol. II, p. 184). Similarly, perhaps, the TRIMs Agreement addresses performance requirements by reference only to national treatment under GATT article III and to prohibitions on quantitative restrictions under GATT article XI (UNCTAD, 1996, vol. I, p. 280).

b. Separate national treatment provision followed by other general standards of treatment clauses

In other cases, the national treatment provision is found in a separate clause from those that relate to other general standards of treatment such as MFN and/or fair and equitable treatment. [17]

Some agreements with separate national treatment and MFN treatment clauses specify also that each contracting party shall accord to investors of the other contracting party or parties the better of national or MFN treatment. NAFTA articles 1102, 1103 and 1104 take such an approach (UNCTAD, 1996, vol. III, p. 74).

c. Combined national and MFN treatment provision

The various general standards of treatment are often included in the same provision of an agreement, though there are variations in drafting. This practice is followed mainly in BITs and in the MAI negotiating text. Three basic models can be identified:

- Some agreements provide for national and MFN treatment in a combined provision without specifying whether one or the other standard should apply in case of conflict between the two. Examples are the German model BIT, article 3 (UNCTAD, 1996, vol. III, p. 169); the Portuguese model BIT, article 3 (2), which combines national and MFN and fair and equitable treatment (UNCTAD, 1998b, p. 268); and the United Kingdom model BIT, article 3 (UNCTAD, 1996, vol. III, p. 187).

- Other agreements specify that the standard which is the "more favourable" to the foreign investor and/or investment, as the case may be, applies: examples include the Swiss model BIT, article 4 (2) (UNCTAD, 1996, vol. III, p. 179); the French model BIT, article 4 "si celui-ci est plus avantageux" (UNCTAD, 1996, vol. III, p. 161); the Netherlands model BIT, article 3 (2); and the MAI negotiating text, part III, "Treatment of Investors" (OECD, 1998b, p. 13).

IIA issues paper series

* The third model provides that the standard that is the "most favourable" to the foreign investor and/or investment, as the case may be, applies; examples include the Chilean model BIT, article 4 (2) (UNCTAD, 1996, vol. III, p. 145); the United States model BIT, article II (1) (UNCTAD, 1996, vol. III, p. 197); and the Energy Charter Treaty, article 10 (7) (UNCTAD, 1996, vol. II, p. 556).

The effects of these variations revolve around the level to which the investor/investment is to be treated vis-à-vis other classes of investors. The first model, by not specifying which standard applies, leaves it to the host country to determine whether to compare the treatment accorded to a foreign investor with domestic or other foreign investors, regardless of which offers better protection. The second and third models differ in that they expressly require the better of national or MFN treatment to apply.

5. Exceptions

The number and scope of exceptions determine the practical effect of national treatment under an investment agreement. The most common approach is to have a wide formulation of the national treatment standard, as described above, followed by exceptions reflecting each contracting party's needs in terms of protecting essential interests. An "opt-out" approach is the more common model, though, as noted above in relation to GATS, an "opt-in" approach is also an option. Exceptions are more frequent where the pre-entry stage is covered. For developing countries, moreover, the question arises whether their special circumstances require special attention through a "development exception". Finally, the question of monitoring of exceptions has arisen in practice.

a. Classification of exceptions

Exceptions to national treatment can be divided into four main categories:

- **General exceptions**. As noted in section I, general exceptions are typically based on public health, order and morals, and national security. Such exceptions are present in many IIAs (and they often appear in a separate provision and apply to all provisions in the agreement, not only to national treatment), as exemplified in the following examples:

  - The OECD National Treatment instrument permits distinctions of treatment for foreign affiliates consistent with the need to maintain public order, the protection of essential security interests and the fulfilment of commitments to maintain international peace and security. The interpretation of these exceptions in concrete situations is left to the member countries, although the need was recognized to apply them with caution, bearing in mind the objectives of the National Treatment instrument; in other words, they should not be used as a general escape clause from the commitments under this instrument (OECD, 1985, p. 16; OECD, 1993, p. 27).

  - NAFTA contains a general national security exception in article 2102 which applies to investment matters. However, as regards exceptions to national treatment, the main approach is to use subject-specific and industry-specific exceptions, discussed below. A similar approach is taken in the Canada-Chile Free Trade Agreement (article O-02, Canada-Chile, 1997).

  - The Energy Charter Treaty contains in article 24 a general exception for the adoption or enforcement of measures necessary to protect human, animal or plant life or health, to the acquisition or distribution of energy materials and products in conditions of short supply, and measures designed to benefit investors who are aboriginal people or socially or economically disadvantaged groups provided that such measures do not constitute a disguised restriction on economic activity in the energy sector or arbitrary or unjustifiable discrimination between contracting parties or investors. The provision goes on to cover protection of essential national security interests (UNCTAD, 1996, vol.II, pp. 566-568).

- The MAI negotiating text contains general exceptions for essential security interests (OECD, 1998b, p. 77).

- GATS, article XIV, provides for exceptions based on the protection of public order and health, while article XIV bis provides for exceptions based on essential security interests (UNCTAD, 1996, vol. I, pp. 299-300).

• **Subject-specific exceptions.** Subject-specific exceptions concern, in particular, the exclusion from national (and MFN) treatment commitments relating to, for example:

- taxation (see, for example, BIT between the Republic of Korea and Mongolia article 7 (b); MAI, article VIII (OECD, 1998b))
- intellectual property rights guaranteed under international intellectual property conventions (United States model BIT, article, II (2) (b), UNCTAD, 1998b, p. 289);
- prudential measures in financial services (BITs signed by Canada; MAI, (OECD, 1998b));
- temporary macroeconomic safeguards (MAI (OECD, 1998b));
- incentives (BIT between Jamaica and the United Kingdom, article 3; NAFTA, article 1108.7 (a));
- public procurement (NAFTA, article 1108.7 (b));
- special formalities in connection with establishment (e.g. information, registration) (NAFTA; United States BITs);
- cultural industries exception (NAFTA, annex 2106); (Muchlinski, 1995, pp. 241, 269).

- **Industry-specific exceptions**. A party may reserve the right to treat domestic and foreign investors in certain types of activities or industries differently under its laws and regulations for reasons of national economic and social policy. This practice appears to have its origins in the United States FCN treaties, and has been followed in the United States BITs, NAFTA, the Canada-Chile Free Trade Agreement and the MAI negotiating text, among others. The most common method of doing so is to "opt out" of the general national treatment obligation, typically by way of an annex of reserved industries and activities which fall outside the scope of the national treatment obligation and in which differential treatment is possible. Under NAFTA, Annex II, each contracting party is allowed to make reservations with respect to specific industries in which the party may adopt more restrictive measures. Exceptions have been made that preserve existing federal measures listed in Annex I to the Agreement. These include, *inter alia*, Mexico's primary energy sector and railroads, United States airlines and radio communications and Canada's cultural industries. Another example of the same approach is provided by the BITs signed by the United States. Thus, for example, the treaty between Grenada and the United States designates in an annex the industries with respect to which each party reserves the right to deny national treatment. The list of industries with respect to Grenada consists of the following: air transportation, government grants, government insurance and loan programmes, ownership of real estate, and use of land and natural resources. The list with respect to the United States is considerably broader and consists of: air transportation, ocean and coastal shipping, banking, insurance, government grants, government insurance and loan programmes, energy and power production, custom house brokers, ownership of real state, ownership and operation of broadcast or common carrier radio and television stations, ownership of shares of the Communications Satellite Corporation, the provision of common carrier telephone and telegraph services, the provision of submarine cable services, and use of land and national resources.[18]

• **Reciprocal national treatment clauses**. In some IIAs the granting of national treatment is contingent upon a reciprocal commitment from the other parties to the same effect. In 1985, the OECD concluded that, where the provision of equal treatment for a foreign affiliate by a host country was conditional on similar treatment being extended to enterprises from the host country in the home country, that constituted an exception to national treatment if it resulted in the foreign affiliate being treated less favourably than similar domestic enterprises (OECD, 1985). In 1993, the OECD declared that reciprocity measures were incompatible with a multilateral approach to liberalization and should be progressively removed (OECD, 1993).

b. *Exceptions based on development considerations*

As noted in the introduction, the standard of national treatment is an important principle for foreign investors, but it may raise difficulties for many host countries, since such treatment may make it difficult to foster the growth of domestic enterprises. This is especially the case for developing countries, since their national enterprises may be particularly vulnerable, especially vis-à-vis large TNCs. Indeed, host Governments sometimes have special policies and programmes that grant advantages and privileges to domestic enterprises in order to stimulate their growth and competitiveness. If a national treatment clause in an IIA obliges a host country to grant the same privileges and benefits to foreign investors, the host Government would in effect be strengthening the ability of foreign investors to compete with local business (UNCTAD, 1998b).

To address this issue, developing countries have at times sought to qualify or limit the application of national treatment in their negotiations through the introduction of a "development clause", in the form of a "development exception", to the general principle of national treatment. Such a "development clause" -- which also reflects the principle that developing countries, by virtue of their weaker economic position and their development needs, should receive special and differential treatment[19] -- serves the purpose of allowing for policy flexibility while maintaining the commitment to the basic principle. For these countries the need to maintain a certain amount of flexibility in the interest of promoting their growth and development is indeed an overriding concern, including when it comes to the application of the national treatment standard.

The industry-specific exceptions discussed above may be based on economic and social development considerations. In other cases, "best efforts" have served the same purpose in, for example, the APEC Non-Binding Investment Principles and in the case of the Energy Charter Treaty for the pre-establishment phase (see above).[20]

It is in this context that, during the negotiations on the draft United Nations Code of Conduct on Transnational Corporations (which was not adopted), a development exception was discussed in relation to national treatment. In particular the developing countries felt that, if the national treatment standard were applied without qualifications, it could prove to be costly to their development efforts in view of the unequal competitive position of domestic enterprises as compared to many TNCs. Accordingly, these countries argued that the national treatment standard should be qualified by a "development clause" which would accord national treatment to TNCs only when the characteristics of those two types of enterprises were the same and the circumstances under which they operated were also similar to those of domestic enterprises (United Nations Commission on Transnational Corporations, 1984, paragraph 27; Asante, 1989, p. 31). Developed countries, for their part, favoured a formulation that was flexible enough to allow preferential treatment for TNCs if the host country should deem this appropriate. The developing countries' views on that point were that, while the question of granting preferential treatment for TNCs was indeed within the sovereign discretion of individual countries, it should not be made a general international standard. Instead, developing countries insisted on the need to allow for preferential treatment to domestic enterprises on account of their development needs. Developed countries indicated that a "development clause" that was too broad and open-ended could undermine the basis of the entire principle.

The "development clause" that came out of these discussions was "without prejudice to measures specified in legislation relating to the declared development objectives of developing countries". More specifically, the last (1990) draft of the Code before negotiations were discontinued, proposed by the Chairperson of the reconvened special session of the Commission on Transnational Corporations, contained the following provision:[21]

> " 50. Subject to national requirements for maintaining public order and protecting national security and consistent with national constitutions and basic laws, and without prejudice to measures specified in legislation relating to the declared development objectives of the developing countries, entities of transnational corporations should be entitled to treatment no less favourable than that accorded to domestic enterprises in similar circumstances" (UN-ECOSOC, 1990, p. 15).

This formulation sought to make national treatment subject to legally specified development measures. It therefore requires a positive legal basis for different treatment by way of an exception to national treatment.

Development considerations of this kind have figured in certain national treatment clauses of BITs, though such a practice appears to have become less common in recent years. For example, Protocol 2 of the BIT between Indonesia and Switzerland allows derogation from national treatment of Swiss investors "in view of the present stage of development of the Indonesian national economy". However, Indonesia would grant "identical or compensating facilities to investments and nationals of the Swiss Confederation in similar economic activities" (UNCTAD, 1998b, p. 64). Similarly, Germany has accepted certain exceptions to national treatment provided these are undertaken for development purposes only, for example the development of small-scale industries, and that the measures do not substantially impair investments from a German investor (UNCTAD, 1998b, p. 64). Jamaica, too, has sought in its BITs to reconcile its growth and development concerns with the needs of foreign investors in reference to the granting of incentives.[22] A recent example of a development clause can be found in the BIT between Italy and Morocco, which provides:

> "Investors of the two Contracting Parties shall not be entitled to national treatment in terms of benefiting from aid, grants, loans, insurance and guarantees accorded by the Government of one of the Contracting Parties exclusively to its own nationals or enterprises within the framework of activities carried out under national development programmes."

c.   *Monitoring*

Regional and multilateral investment agreements sometimes provide for a mechanism to follow up on the implementation of the agreement in question and, in particular, to ensure transparency of exceptions and/or to administer the gradual abolition of exceptions or time-derogations to the application of the national treatment. Perhaps the most tested mechanism in this respect is the OECD Committee on International Investment and Multinational Enterprises (CIME). It has undertaken periodic surveys of member country measures that constitute exceptions to the "national treatment" principle, based upon its clarifying interpretations of the 1976 Declaration. The Committee has considered the application of national treatment in five main areas: investment by established foreign affiliates, official aids and subsidies, tax obligations, government purchasing and public contracts, and access to local bank credits and the capital market. These are the principal areas in which the OECD member States have passed laws and regulations providing for different treatment for foreign affiliates.[23] Under the 1991 Review of the OECD Declaration, the application of national treatment to the privatization of enterprises previously under public ownership was taken up. The Committee considered that access to the areas newly opened up by such a policy should be on a non-discriminatory basis between private domestic and foreign affiliates already established in the country in question. Any restrictions applying to foreign affiliates should be reported as exceptions to national treatment (OECD, 1992, p. 27).

In order to assist the Committee in its work, the Third Revised Council Decision on National Treatment introduced a new requirement that member countries should notify to the Committee all measures constituting exceptions to the principle of national treatment. Thereupon the Committee is empowered to examine the notification. Furthermore, a member country may refer another member country to the Committee where the former considers itself to have been prejudiced by the introduction of measures by the latter. The Committee is also available as a forum for consultations, on the invitation of a member country, on any matter related to the implementation of the Declaration (OECD, 1994; Muchlinski, 1995, p. 584).

The TRIMs Agreement provides another example of a follow up mechanism in relation to the implementation of the Agreement. Pursuant to article 7 of the Agreement, a Committee on Trade-Related Investment Measures was established with a view to carrying out the responsibilities assigned to it by the WTO Council for Trade in Goods and to afford members the opportunity to consult on any matters relating to the operation and implementation of the TRIMs Agreement (article 7, 2). More specifically, the Committee is entrusted with the task of monitoring the operation and implementation of the Agreement and reporting thereon annually to the Council for Trade in Goods (article 7, 3). Moreover, according to article 8, the provisions of article XXII and article XXIII of GATT 1994, as elaborated by the Dispute Settlement Understanding, also apply to consultations and settlement of disputes under the TRIMS Agreement.

Monitoring mechanisms have often served to resolve implementation difficulties, as they provide a vehicle to explore flexible options.

Notes

[1]   In fact, until the 1990s, China did not agree to incorporate the national treatment standard in BITs as a matter of principle, although it was granted in the BITs between China and Germany (article 3 (IV)) and China and the United

Kingdom (article 3) (Denza and Brooks, 1987). Since the early 1990s, as China pursued its economic reforms and continued to open up to the outside world -- with a view towards attracting more FDI -- it began to provide national treatment in BITs, but with certain qualifications. The most important qualification is that national treatment shall be limited by national laws and regulations; such qualification appears in, for example, the BIT between China and Morocco (article 3 (1)). In some recent BITs concluded by China (e.g. the BIT between China and the Republic of Korea (article 3 (2)), the national treatment standard appears without qualifications. In 1996, the State Council of the Government of China declared its policy of according foreign investors full national treatment on a gradual basis.

2   See, for example, the BIT between Denmark and Indonesia. The Draft United Nations Code of Conduct on Transnational Corporations refers to "entities of transnational corporations" (UNCTAD, 1996).

3   The AALCC prepared three draft model BITs intended to provide possible negotiating texts for consideration by the countries of the region. Model A is a draft BIT patterned on the agreements entered into between some of the countries of the region with industrialized States, with certain changes and improvements particularly on the matter of promotion of investments. Model B reflects an agreement whose provisions are somewhat more restrictive in the matter of the protection of investment and contemplates a degree of flexibility in regard to admission and protection of investment. Model C reflects an agreement on the pattern of Model A but applicable to specific classes of investment only, as determined by the host State.

4   See for example the BIT between Jamaica and the United Kingdom (article 3).

5   For example, the BITs between Egypt and Jamaica, Argentina and Morocco, Niger and Tunisia.

6   See further Pattison (1983, pp. 318-319) for a discussion of the Egypt-United States BIT in this respect (it should be noted that the Egypt-United States BIT was renegotiated in recent years).

7   See further Eden (1996); and Gestrin and Rugman (1994, 1996). See also the Canada-Chile Free Trade Agreement (5 December 1996, Chapter G, articles G-01 to G-08) for similar provisions (Canada and Chile, 1997).

8   However, MFN treatment is limited to investors and investments from other member States, so as to ensure that investors and investments from non-member States cannot benefit from measures aimed only at investors and investments from member States (ASEAN, 1998).

9   The GATS applies to trade in services, defined in article I as the supply of services through any of four modes: cross-border trade, consumption abroad,

commercial presence and presence of natural persons. The third mode of supply (commercial presence) is the one that mostly concerns investment policies and regulations. It involves the supply of a service through the establishment of an entity (which may or may not have juridical personality, e.g. a subsidiary or a branch). This section focuses mainly on how national treatment applies to mode 3 of the GATS.

10   See, for example, the BITs signed by the United States with Costa Rica, Armenia and Argentina.

11   See also Raby, 1990, pp. 410-411, on the similar provision, article 1604, of the Canada-United States Free Trade Agreement.

12   As noted earlier, the term "affecting" has been interpreted to bring within the scope of GATS any measure that affects, whether directly or indirectly, the supply of a service. This would include not only investment-related measures but also all other aspects of domestic regulation that affect the operations of a service supplying entity. For example, in the case of an accounting firm, a national treatment obligation would cover all measures relating to the establishment of the firm (the investment) as well as all other regulations affecting its operations (e.g. qualification requirements, licensing requirements, technical standards for accounting).

13   The same functional formulation is used in the United Kingdom model BIT, article 3 (2), in relation to the protection of investors (UNCTAD, 1996, vol. III, p. 187).

14   It has been argued that inclusion of the phrase "in like circumstances" in the MAI was especially relevant in order to ensure that the national treatment standard would not interfere with a party's ability to take measures for environmental purposes.

15   The use of the word "same" or the term "as favourable as" may be seen as synonymous in practice.

16   However, preferential treatment for Arab investors vis-à-vis other foreign investors is possible at the discretion of the host country on the grounds specified in article 16 of the Agreement (UNCTAD, 1996, vol. II, p. 217).

17   Examples of separate national treatment provisions followed by other general standards of treatment clauses are: NAFTA, articles 1102-1103; Canada-Chile Free Trade Agreement, articles G-02-G-03; TRIPS Agreement, articles 3-4; GATS, articles II, XVII; and AALCC Model BITs, articles 4-5.

18   The list of national treatment and MFN treatment exceptions may differ considerably. For example, in the annex to the BIT between Jamaica and the United States, the United States identifies 17 exceptions to MFN and Jamaica identifies four. With respect to national treatment, the United States identifies 13 exceptions and Jamaica only one.

[19]   This principle has been recognized, for example, in the Set of Multilaterally Agreed Equitable Principles and Rules for the Control of Restrictive Business Practices.

[20]   The ECT however provided for future conclusion of a supplementary agreement that would accord national treatment during the pre-establishment phase on a binding basis. (See the discussion above.)

[21]   That text of the draft Code of Conduct was submitted by the Chairperson of the reconvened special session of the Commission on Transnational Corporations to the President of the Economic and Social Council. In his letter to the President, the Chairperson indicated *inter alia* that the text of the draft Code represented an effort to facilitate compromise while preserving the texts already agreed *ad referendum*, and added that "the Bureau considers that the work of the reconvened special session of the Commission on Transnational Corporations has been concluded and it is the Chairperson's impression that the text annexed will receive the support of the overwhelming majority of countries from all regions" (UN-ECOSOC, 1990, p. 1).

[22]   See the 1990 Jamaica-Switzerland BIT, art. 3; and the 1991 Jamaica-Netherlands BIT, art. 3(6). A similar approach is contained in the BIT between Denmark and Indonesia (article 3).

[23]   The Committee has also considered the area of nationality requirements for example the requirement that a certain number of members of the board of a company must possess the nationality of the host State (OECD, 1985, pp. 20-34; OECD, 1993, pp. 28-47).

Section III

INTERACTION WITH OTHER ISSUES AND CONCEPTS

National treatment has the potential to interact with all other provisions of an IIA (table 1). Indeed, the United Kingdom model BIT, in article 3 (3), expressly states that, " [f]or the avoidance of doubt it is confirmed that the treatment provided for in paragraphs (1) and (2) above [national and MFN treatment] shall apply to

Table 1. Interaction across issues and concepts

Concepts in other papers	National treatment
Scope and definition	++
Admission and establishment	++
Incentives	++
Investment-related trade measures	+
Most-favoured-nation treatment	++
Fair and equitable treatment	++
Taxation	++
Transfer pricing	0
Competition	++
Transfer of technology	+
Employment	++
Social responsibility	++
Environment	0
Home country measures	0
Host country operational measures	++
Illicit payments	+
Taking of property	++
State contracts	+
Funds transfer	+
Transparency	++
Dispute settlement (investor-State)	++
Dispute settlement (State-State)	0
Modalities and implementation	+

Source: UNCTAD.
Key: 0   =   negligible or no interaction.
          +   =   moderate interaction.
          ++ =   extensive interaction.

Articles 1 to 11 of this Agreement" (UNCTAD, 1998b, p. 281). This affirms the applicability of, *inter alia,* national treatment to all substantive provisions for the United Kingdom model BIT.

The following interactions, in particular, should be highlighted:

*   **Scope and definition.** Given that the definitions of terms such as "investment" and "investor" determine the types of transactions, assets and activities to which the substantive provisions of an agreement apply, these terms interact strongly with national treatment in that they specify the beneficiaries of the standard on the basis of the subject matter of the agreement. In principle, the principal beneficiaries of national treatment are "investors" and "investments". Thus, national treatment can apply to those assets and/or transactions and/ or entities that are specified in the definition provision. For example, if the definition of "investment" does not include portfolio investment, the national treatment standard does not apply to this type of investment. (See also UNCTAD, 1999d.) With respect to the definition of "investor", an important issue here is the definition of the nationality of firms, since this would determine which enterprises are entitled to national treatment under a particular agreement. It is also a matter of practical importance to differentiate whether a foreign affiliate is entitled to national treatment under the provisions of an international agreement, or its treatment derives from its status as a "national firm" under the host country laws on nationality.

*   **Admission and establishment.** As noted in section II, there is a strong interaction between the provision on national treatment and those dealing with admission and establishment of investments where an agreement extends national treatment protection to the pre-entry phase of the investment process (see also UNCTAD, 1999c). In such cases, national treatment operates to ensure that treatment of prospective foreign investors with respect to admission conditions, requirements and promotional measures is based on national treatment, as defined in the applicable IIA.

• **Incentives.** Where national treatment extends to incentives, the standard interacts closely with the incentive provisions as it seeks to ensure that incentives are available to foreign investors on terms equal to, or no less favourable than, those enjoyed by domestic investors of the host country. However, where preferential treatment is sought regarding eligibility for incentives for domestic investors, then exceptions to national treatment may be required. Equally, where special incentives are available to foreign investors only, national treatment has no role to play, although the MFN standard may be invoked to ensure no differences of treatment as between different foreign investors.

• **MFN treatment.** The interactions between national treatment and MFN are extensive and have been partly discussed in section II. (See also UNCTAD, 1999b, pp. 30-32.) For the purposes of this paper, it may be noted that national treatment alone might be insufficient to exclude possible differences of treatment accorded to foreign investors from different home countries. Thus, where certain foreign investors are granted preferential treatment, MFN ensures that such treatment extends to other foreign investors, unless they are expressly excluded from MFN by way of an exception in the applicable IIA. Furthermore, it should also be noted that exceptions to MFN are less frequent than to national treatment, as it may be easier for host countries to treat foreign investors from various countries equally than to treat foreign and domestic investors equally. Finally, where national treatment is accorded only to certain classes of foreign investors, as may be the case for investors from other member countries of a regional economic integration organization (REIO), MFN may have to be specifically excepted so as to avoid "free rider" problems; otherwise foreign investors from non-member countries might demand national treatment without assuming the mutual obligations associated with REIO membership. This would be the case particularly in relation to regional economic agreements that extend national treatment to the pre-entry stage (Karl, 1996).

In essence, the effect of an MFN provision in an IIA on a national treatment provision in another IIA is to raise all other country signatories of the first IIA to the standard of national treatment guarantee in the second IIA. Thus, while some IIAs do not explicitly include a promise of national treatment, parties may still be obligated to provide national treatment by virtue of the MFN provision. Occasionally, a country has included a guarantee of national treatment in an earlier IIA that it does not wish to extend to any other country through an MFN treatment clause. The interaction of MFN and national treatment provisions is therefore of special importance and requires careful wording.

- **Fair and equitable treatment.** National treatment and fair and equitable treatment often co-exist in an investment agreement. (See also UNCTAD, 1999a.) Fair and equitable treatment and national treatment complement each other in various ways, with the former providing a broad objective test to resolve doubtful situations regarding eligibility for national treatment.

- **Taxation.** Significant interactions occur in this field in that most tax treaties apply national treatment to the taxation of foreign investors operating in the host country (UNCTAD, 1998a, p. 87). On the other hand, as noted in section II, IIAs often exclude taxation from the operation of national treatment.

- **Employment.** As noted in section II, a standard similar to that of national treatment is used in the ILO Tripartite Declaration on Multinational Enterprises and Social Policy as one of the standards for determining the legitimacy of TNC practices in relation to terms and conditions of employment and industrial relations. In this respect, TNCs which observe the same standards as domestic employers in the same industry would have fulfilled only the minimum requirements under this voluntary code. However, national treatment is used here in a very specific manner. It is not the treatment of investors that is governed by the standard;

rather it is used (here, and in the following paragraph) to specify their obligations.

- **Social responsibility.** As foreign investors are granted rights similar to those of domestic investors (national treatment), they may also be bound by similar obligations. As with employment issues, so also wider issues of the social responsibility of TNCs can be made subject to national standards. Thus, a TNC may be seen as acting in accordance with its obligations to observe certain social policies in the host country if it operates in the same manner as domestic enterprises in the same industry or sector. However, for reasons of policy, the host country may require different standards of responsibility from domestic and foreign enterprises, for example where more onerous social responsibilities are imposed on the latter.

- **Host country operational measures.** National treatment has close interactions with the issue of host country operational measures since operational conditions that apply to foreign investors and not to domestic investors are, in principle, inconsistent with the national treatment standard.

- **Taking of property.** IIAs typically recognize the international-law-based right of a host State to expropriate foreign property within its territory, provided that such expropriation meets certain requirements, including that it does not discriminate between foreign and local investors. A provision of national treatment would seem to reinforce the obligation of the host country not to discriminate between local and foreign investors on matters of expropriation. Moreover, for the purposes of compensation, a distinction is usually made between an expropriation of foreign-owned property and loss caused by armed conflict. In the former case, the standard of compensation usually relates to the full market value of the expropriated assets at the date of expropriation. In the latter case, most BITs provide that compensation for this kind of loss should be given to the foreign investor on the basis of the MFN standard, though some agreements refer to national treatment (UNCTAD, 1998b, p. 73). This issue has led to disputes before ICSID between investors and host countries as to the precise nature of the latter's obligations (ICSID, 1990, 1997).

- **Transparency.** A vital aspect of national treatment is to ensure that foreign investors are fully informed of the laws, regulations and administrative practices that apply to their operations. Such matters may be better known to domestic investors. It is implicit in the national treatment standard that such information imbalances be eliminated. Equally, transparency may require that exceptions to national treatment are clearly reported so that foreign investors are aware of them. This practice is followed, for example, under the OECD National Treatment instrument (OECD, 1993) and in the TRIMs Agreement (Article 6, UNCTAD, 1996, vol. I, p. 281).

- **Dispute settlement (investor-State).** National treatment interacts with dispute settlement issues in that it requires that a foreign investor be given access to national dispute settlement mechanisms on at least the same terms as national investors. However, where international means of investor-to-State dispute settlement are available, the principle of national treatment does not apply since such facilities are generally not available to national investors. Investor-to-State dispute settlement mechanisms may therefore be considered an exception to national treatment in favour of foreign investors.

The important interactions between the national treatment provision and many other provisions underscore the significance that the principle has in international investment relations. In drawing up IIAs, therefore, special attention needs to be given to this standard.

CONCLUSION: ECONOMIC AND DEVELOPMENT IMPLICATIONS AND POLICY OPTIONS

National treatment may be interpreted as formal equality of treatment between foreign and domestic enterprises. Indeed, such a perception may be reinforced in an IIA, given the formal equality or "legal symmetry" of the parties. However, where countries at different levels of development are parties to an IIA, such formal equality may disregard important differences in the actual situation and capabilities of the enterprises on each side. The formal "legal symmetry" of their legal situation may be accompanied by actual "economic asymmetry" (UNCTAD, 1999e).[1] In such a context, application of the national treatment standard may require more than formal equality, so that the development needs of a developing country party to an IIA are taken into account in the definition and application of the standard.

While there is no doubt that national treatment is an important principle for foreign investors, its actual implementation may cause difficulties for host developing countries. In particular, there is a risk that economically strong foreign firms may impede or distort the development of domestic enterprises in a host country. Effective competition regulations may counter anti-competitive behaviour of TNCs (UNCTAD, 1997). However, such regulations cannot deal with effects arising from the mere presence of powerful firms with better access to finance, technology, skills and markets. This may call for special policies to help domestic firms, bearing in mind the spillover effects that TNCs can have in respect to the development of local suppliers and the upgrading of domestic competitors (UNCTAD, 1999f). There is thus a trade-off between offering national treatment as a means of increasing FDI inflows, and circumscribing national treatment as a means of promoting local enterprise development. How this trade-off is made depends on the conditions, levels of development and objectives of each host country.

The discretion of central and local governmental agencies to pursue development strategies may be unnecessarily curtailed by the fear that differential treatment of domestic firms could jeopardize the national treatment principle. As a result, otherwise useful policies and programmes might never be attempted, and existing development schemes favouring local firms and other bodies abandoned (Nurick, 1998; World Development Movement, 1998).

At the same time, strategies for enhancing the development dimension in respect of national treatment need to be woven into the liberalization process that many host countries have undertaken. Thus, there is no point in simply proposing a strategy in respect of national treatment, for example exceptions to national treatment to protect and promote certain domestic industries, without going through the exercise of testing their effectiveness in the broader context of liberalization. In a real sense, the liberalization phenomenon has become the principal touchstone of the efficacy of strategies to enhance the development dimension in respect of national treatment or indeed in respect of any other aspect of an investment regime. But of course it assumes greater significance in respect of national treatment by reason of the predominant position that that standard has among others, not only in economic and political terms but also in psychological terms, that is, the effect on national psyche.

In light of the above, a measure of balance and flexibility may be appropriate to ensure that formal equality of treatment does not become the basis for de facto better treatment for foreign investors, while at the same time ensuring that foreign investors are treated equally in like situations. In order to achieve this, a number of options arise, discussed below.

A. Option 1: no national treatment provision

As noted in section II, one option is to conclude IIAs that do not provide for national treatment. The purpose of this option is to avoid equality of treatment between national and foreign investors for a host country with strong reservations about limiting its freedom to offer preferential treatment to domestic firms for certain purposes. This approach is the most restrictive in terms of investors' rights and the most respectful in terms of host country discretion. Agreements enshrining this approach are not frequent.

B. Option 2: national treatment provision

There are a number of ways in which a national treatment clause can be granted. In each case the general exceptions mentioned in section II apply, in line with the common practice in many IIAs. However, before outlining those ways, some general questions on the national treatment standard must be raised because, in a real sense, the kernel of the question lies in the efficient and transparent use and application of exceptions to national treatment. In this, national treatment is quite different from MFN, where fewer exceptions are likely (UNCTAD, 1999b, pp. 26, 31).

Do exceptions to national treatment promote economic development and growth for developing countries? This should be assessed in the context of current pressures towards liberalization. In particular, where national treatment is granted at the pre-entry stage, this could prove threatening to national investors if it were to be an unqualified standard. Thus, national treatment in the establishment of an investment is seldom, if ever, granted without exceptions thereto (UNCTAD, 1999c). These usually relate to infant industries that need special treatment if they are to develop, or to other such cases.

Secondly, do exceptions to national treatment operate as a disincentive for inward investment? This question needs to be analysed on a case-by-case basis, in the context of other FDI determinants (UNCTAD, 1998a). In every case, caution and fairness must be exercised to avoid unnecessary exceptions that serve only to protect inefficient firms or industries, and that may signal an unwelcoming investment climate to foreign investors. In any event, the use of exceptions would need to meet transparency standards.

Thirdly, should exceptions be phased so that they operate only for a transitional period? This has the advantage of giving a period of grace to a developing country. During this period, the country can ensure the conditions compatible with granting national treatment in the future. However, even a transitional period may not be enough if development targets have not been attained by the end of the period. Thus, positive measures (e.g. technical assistance) might be required to achieve this objective. However, time limits may not be appropriate for all exceptions, e.g. those involving national security or the continuing importance of particular industries.

Fourthly, should exceptions be structured on the basis of the GATS type "opt-in" or "positive list" approach or the NAFTA type "opt-out" or "negative list" approach? The former may be preferable where gradual liberalization is sought. By contrast, the "opt-out" approach may have certain disadvantages: this approach may curtail the ability of a host country to distinguish between domestic and foreign investments as it may be difficult to identify with precision all the industries and activities to which national treatment should not apply.

Against this background the basic policy variations are as follows:

1.   Post-establishment national treatment

*   **Option 2.a: limited post-establishment national treatment with strong host country authority.** This option preserves the strongest host country discretion while offering national treatment to foreign investments and/or investors at the post-entry stage. It could be used by host countries that may wish to offer a degree of national treatment without limiting their regulatory powers too greatly. Its principal features include some or all of the following:

    *   Application to post-establishment treatment only, thereby preserving the right to treat domestic and foreign investors differently at the point of entry, e.g. through screening laws and operational conditions on admission (see further UNCTAD, 1999a).

    *   A development exception in the form of a development clause in the context of the declared development

objectives of a host country. It may be arguable that, in view of the factual test of "same circumstances" (or even "like situations" or "like circumstances"), a development exception may not be needed, as the situation for foreign and domestic firms in developing countries may not be comparable. However, this may not be an adequate safeguard, as it could equally be argued that, if both types of firms compete in the same market, then preferential treatment for a domestic firm could be construed as an exception to national treatment. Therefore, to ensure that a developing host country has the discretion to assist its emerging firms, an express exception may be the surest way of proceeding in the context of an IIA. As a development clause is potentially quite wide in its scope of application, the wide discretion it reserves for a developing host country could be seen as creating uncertainty as to when and where national treatment actually applies and therefore would not be regarded favourably by foreign investors. Clear lists of excepted or included industries or activities offer greater certainty.

Short of a general exception for development, provision can be made for a national treatment exception in respect of special incentives granted by a host country only to its nationals and companies, especially for the purpose of stimulating local enterprise development.

• Exception of specific industries, activities and/or policy measures from the standard of national treatment.

• The substantive test of national treatment is limited to:

- the "same" circumstances, thereby avoiding wider comparisons based on "like" circumstances;
- the "same treatment", thereby avoiding the possibility of treatment more favourable to the foreign investor that can arise from the formulation "no less favourable".

- An exception for political subdivisions and/or local government measures, as appropriate, reflecting the internal political organization of the host country.

- Limitation to *de jure* national treatment only, thereby allowing for *de facto* differentiation in the treatment of foreign investors.

- A stand alone national treatment clause without reference to other standards such as MFN or fair and equitable treatment.

The principal development implication of this approach is its flexibility in terms of preserving host country discretion. On the other hand, this approach may be perceived by foreign investors as not offering adequate levels of protection against differential treatment -- in principle, as well as when it comes to the administration of a provision with extensive discretion.

- **Option 2.b: full post-establishment national treatment.** This option offers a higher standard of national treatment for the foreign investor and limits the discretion of the host country to treat national and foreign investors differently. Its principal features include some or all of the following:

  - Application to post-establishment treatment only.

  - A minimal number of exceptions based on specific industries or activities seen as vital to national economic policy, and/or that need protection to survive on the basis of infant industry concerns.

  - The substantive test of national treatment is extended to:
    - "like" circumstances, allowing for the application of national treatment to similar, though not necessarily identical, situations;
    - "no less favourable treatment", thereby allowing for better treatment of foreign investors;

- nothing is said as to whether or not national treatment applies to specified activities or factual situations or circumstances.

• No exception for political subdivisions and/or local government measures.

• Application of national treatment *de jure* and *de facto*, thereby ensuring both formal and informal protection for foreign investors.

• A national treatment clause that coexists with, or incorporates within its text, the better of several standards of treatment such as MFN or fair and equitable treatment.

The development implications of this approach are that a host country extends the application of post-entry national treatment disciplines to as wide a range of situations as possible.

The following options add national treatment at the pre-establishment phase to national treatment at the post-establishment stage as described above.

2. Pre-establishment national treatment

• **Option 2c: limited pre-establishment national treatment.** In this option, national treatment extends to pre-establishment as well as post-establishment treatment, thereby limiting a host country's discretion as regards the entry of foreign investors. But the host country still retains some degree of control over the extent and pace of the liberalization of limitations and conditions of entry. (For further discussion, see UNCTAD, 1999c.) It would be an option for a host country that wishes to liberalize investment entry in its economy at a gradual pace. Its principal features may include one of the following two main variations:

  • Use of an "opt-in" or "positive list" approach à la GATS. No industry and/or activity is made subject to national treatment at the pre-establishment phase until and unless it is specifically agreed upon by the host country.

- A "best endeavours" option such as that used in the APEC Non-Binding Investment Principles so that developing countries are not legally bound to grant national treatment at the pre-establishment phase. In a variation of this option, a best endeavours provision could be coupled with a commitment to grant (or negotiate) legally binding national treatment at the pre-establishment phase at a later stage (as done in the Energy Charter Treaty). This has the advantage of allowing a transitional period for developing countries before they become subject to national treatment disciplines. Its disadvantage is that it involves uncertainty before entry for foreign investors in the short to medium term, which could act as a disincentive; it may also encourage some investors to refrain from investing in order to await the new instrument.

- **Option 2d**: full pre-establishment national treatment. Under this option, a host country's commitment to grant national treatment on entry extends in principle to all foreign investors unless such investment is to take place in activities or industries specifically excluded by the host country in a treaty. This option narrows considerably the discretion of a host country, since it can only use its prerogative to exclude specific activities from the operation of the standard at the time an agreement is completed.

Such a policy choice limits to a considerable extent a host country's traditional right to control the entry of aliens into its territory. It may be of value where a host country Government considers that a number of industries or activities can benefit from increased openness and from a more competitive market environment. At the same time, a host country may protect certain industries or activities by way of a "negative list", although this involves a difficult assessment as to which industries or activities need such special treatment. Failure to include an industry or activity may result in it being subjected to potentially damaging competition from foreign investors, especially where an IIA contains a standstill commitment on further restrictive policies. This would prevent a host country from including industries or activities in a "negative list" in the future.

* * *

As with the post-establishment options noted above, pre-establishment national treatment may be broader or narrower, depending on the wording of the principle and the use of various qualifications indicated earlier.

3. Combinations

• **Option 2e: hybrid.** This option involves various combinations of the elements of post and pre-establishment national treatment to produce a compromise between the various possibilities outlined above. For example, different permutations of the substantive test of differential treatment could also be devised, resulting in wider or narrower application of national treatment. Other matters open to variation from the above options include *de jure* and *de facto* differential treatment; the degree of interaction between national treatment and MFN and fair and equitable treatment; and the extent to which subnational entities are subjected to national treatment disciplines.

There is little point in attempting to list all the various permutations under this heading, as the outcome depends on a process of negotiation in the light of specific circumstances. The range of permutations can be gleaned from the various alternative formulations reviewed in section II above. In fact, the options indicated above are merely analytical constructs whose principal purpose is to indicate broad -- but hypothetical -- approaches to the subject.

Note

1   Economic asymmetry is illustrated by BITs in which one developing country partner will in practice operate only as a capital-importing country, so that its rights under the treaty as a home country may not mean much in reality.

REFERENCES

Asante, S.K.B. (1989). "The concept of good corporate citizen in international business", *ICSID Review - Foreign Investment Law Journal*, vol. 4 (Spring), pp. 1-38.

Association of South-East Asian Nations (ASEAN) (1998). "Framework Agreement on the ASEAN Investment Area", http://www.asean.or.id/economic/aem/30/frm_aia.htm.

Canada and Chile (1997). "Free trade agreement", *International Legal Materials*, vol. 36, pp. 1067-1192.

Denza, Eileen and Shelagh Brooks (1987). "Investment protection treaties: United Kingdom experience", *International and Comparative Law Quarterly*, vol. 36 (Fall), pp. 908-923.

Dolzer, Rudolf and Margrete Stevens (1995). *Bilateral Investment Treaties* (The Hague: Martinus Nijhoff).

Eden, Lorraine (1996). "The emerging North American investment regime", *Transnational Corporations* 5, 3 (December), pp. 61-98.

European Union (EU) 1997. "Treaty of Amsterdam", http://ue.eu.int/Amsterdam/en/amsteroc/en/treaty/main.htm.

Fatouros, A., ed. (1993). *Transnational Corporations: The International Legal Framework*, United Nations Library on Transnational Corporations, vol. 20 (London and New York: Routledge on behalf of the United Nations).

Gestrin, Michael and Alan M. Rugman (1994). "The North American Free Trade Agreement and foreign direct investment", *Transnational Corporations*, 3, 1 (February), pp. 77-95.

_____ (1996). "The NAFTA investment provisions: prototype for multilateral investment rules?", in OECD, *Market Access After the Uruguay Round* (Paris: OECD), pp. 63-78.

International Centre for Settlement of Investment Disputes (ICSID) (1972--). *Investment Treaties* (Dobbs Ferry: Oceana).

_____ (1990). "Asian Agricultural Products Ltd (AAPL) v. Republic of Sri Lanka", *International Legal Materials*, vol. 30, pp. 577-655.

_____ (1997). "American Manufacturing and Trading Inc. v. Republic of Zaire", *International Legal Materials*, vol. 36, pp. 1534-1561.

Jackson, J.H. (1997). *The World Trading System: Law and Policy of International Economic Relations*, 2nd ed. (Cambridge: MIT Press).

Karl, Joachim (1996). "Multilateral investment agreements and regional economic integration", *Transnational Corporations*, 5, 2 (August), pp. 19-50.

Mattoo, A. (1997). "National treatment in the GATS: corner-stone or pandora's box?" *Journal of World Trade*, 31, pp. 107-135.

Muchlinski, Peter T. (1995). *Multinational Enterprises and the Law* (Oxford: Blackwell Publishers).

Netherlands (1997). "Agreement on encouragement and reciprocal protection of investments between and the Kingdom of the Netherlands", March 1997 (rev. 2), mimeo..

Nurick, R. (1998). "The multilateral agreement on investment: potential impacts on local economic development and poverty issues in the UK" (London:Oxfam), mimeo..

Organisation for Economic Co-operation and Development (OECD) (1985). *National Treatment for Foreign-Controlled Enterprises* (Paris: OECD).

IIA issues paper series

_____ (1992). *The OECD Declaration and Decisions on International Investment and Multinational Enterprises: 1991 Review* (Paris: OECD).

_____ (1993). *National Treatment for Foreign-Controlled Enterprises* (Paris: OECD).

_____ (1994). *National Treatment for Foreign-Controlled Enterprises* (Paris: OECD) Working Papers, vol. II, No. 34.

_____ (1998b). "The MAI Negotiating Text (as of 24 April 1998)", http://www.oecd.org/daf/cims/mai/negtext.htm.

Pattison, Joseph (1983). "The United States-Egypt bilateral investment treaty: a prototype for future negotiation", *Cornell International Law Journal*, 16, pp. 305-339.

Raby, J. (1990). "The investment provisions of the Canada-United States free trade agreement: a Canadian perspective", *American Journal of International Law*, vol. 84, pp. 394-443.

United Nations (1950). "General Agreement on Tariffs and Trade", *United Nations Treaty Series*, vol. 55, pp. 194-307.

_____ (1972). "Paris Convention for the Protection of Industrial Property of March 20, 1883", *United Nations Treaty Series*, vol. 828, pp. 305-388.

United Nations Centre on Transnational Corporations (UNCTC) (1990a). *Key Concepts in International Investment Arrangements and Their Relevance to Negotiations on International Transactions in Services* (New York: United Nations), United Nations publication, Sales No. E. 90.II.A.3.

_____ (1990b). *Transnational Corporations, Services and the Uruguay Round* (New York: United Nations) United Nations publication, Sales No. E.90.II.A.11.

United Nations Commission on Transnational Corporations (1984). "Outstanding issues in the draft Code of Conduct on Transnational Corporations" (New York: United Nations), United Nations document, E/C.10/1984/S/5, mimeo..

United Nations Conference on Trade and Development (UNCTAD) (1994). *World Investment Report 1994: Transnational Corporations, Employment and the Workplace* (New York and Geneva: United Nations), United Nations publication, Sales No.E.94.II.A.14.

_____ (1996). *International Investment Instruments: A Compendium, vol. I, II and III* (New York and Geneva: United Nations), United Nations publications, Sales Nos. E.96.II.A.9, 10, 11.

_____ (1997). *World Investment Report 1997: Transnational Corporations, Market Structure and Competition Policy* (New York and Geneva: United Nations), United Nations publication, Sales No.E.97.II.D.10.

_____ (1998a). *World Investment Report: Trends and Determinants* (New York and Geneva: United Nations), United Nations publication, Sales No.E.98.II.D.5.

_____ (1998b). *Bilateral Investment Treaties in the Mid-1990s* (New York and Geneva: United Nations), United Nations publication, Sales No.E.98.II.D.8.

_____ (1999a). *Fair and Equitable Treatment. UNCTAD Series on Issues in International Investment Agreements* (New York and Geneva: United Nations), United Nations publication, Sales No. E.99.II.D.00.

_____ (1999b). *Most-Favoured-Nation Treatment. UNCTAD Series on Issues in International Investment Agreements* (New York and Geneva: United Nations), United Nations publication, Sales No. E.99.II.D.11.

_____ (1999c). *Admission and Establishment. UNCTAD Series on Issues in International Investment Agreements* (New York and Geneva: United Nations), United Nations publication, Sales No. E.99.II.D.10.

_____ (1999d). *Scope and Definition. UNCTAD Series on Issues in International Investment Agreements* (New York and Geneva: United Nations), United Nations publication, Sales No. E.99.II.D.9.

_____ (1999e). "International investment agreements: concepts allowing for a certain flexibility in the interest of promoting growth and development" (Geneva: United Nations), United Nations document, TD/B/COM.2/EM.5/2, mimeo.

_____(1999f). *Foreign Direct Investment and Development. UNCTAD Series on Issues in International Investment Agreements.* (New York and Geneva: United Nations), United Nations publication, Sales No. E.98.II.D.15.

United Nations, Economic and Social Council (UN-ECOSOC) (1990). "Development and economic co-operation: transnational corporations" (New York: United Nations), United Nations document, E/1990/94, mimeo..

VerLoren van Themaat, P. (1981). *The Changing Structure of International Economic Law* (Dordrecht: Martinus Nijhoff).

World Bank (1992). *Legal Framework for the Treatment of Foreign Investment, Volume 1: Survey of Existing Instruments* (Washington, DC: World Bank).

World Development Movement (1998). "The impact of the Multilateral Agreement on Investment on local government in the UK" (London: WDM), mimeo.

Selected UNCTAD publications on transnational corporations and foreign direct investment

A. IIA Issues Paper Series

Fair and Equitable Treatment. UNCTAD Series on issues in international investment agreements. 64p. Sales No. E.99.II.D.15. $12.

Investment-Related Trade Measures. UNCTAD Series on issues in international investment agreements. 64p. Sales No. E.99.II.D.12. $12.

Most-Favoured-Nation Treatment. UNCTAD Series on issues in international investment agreements. 72p. Sales No. E.99.II.D.11. $12.

Admission and Establishment. UNCTAD Series on issues in international investment agreements. 72p. Sales No. E.99.II.D.10. $12.

Scope and Definition. UNCTAD Series on issues in international investment agreements. 96p. Sales No. E.99.II.D.9. $12.

Transfer Pricing. UNCTAD Series on issues in international investment agreements. 72p. Sales No. E.99.II.D.8. $12.

Foreign Direct Investment and Development. UNCTAD Series on issues in international investment agreements. 88p. Sales No. E.98.II.D.15. $12.

B. Individual studies

The Financial Crisis in Asia and Foreign Direct Investment: An Assessment. 101 p. Sales No. GV.E.98.0.29. $20.

World Investment Report 1998: Trends and Determinants. 430 p. Sales No. E.98.II.D.5. $45.

World Investment Report 1998: Trends and Determinants. An Overview. 67 p. Free-of-charge.

Bilateral Investment Treaties in the mid-1990s. 314 p. Sales No. E.98.II.D.8. $46.

Handbook on Foreign Direct Investment by Small and Medium-sized Enterprises: Lessons from Asia. 200 p. Sales No. E.98.II.D.4. $48.

Handbook on Foreign Direct Investment by Small and Medium-sized Enterprises: Lessons from Asia. Executive Summary and Report on the Kunming Conference. 74 p. Free-of-charge.

International Investment Towards the Year 2002. 166 p. Sales No. GV.E.98.0.15. $29. (Joint publication with Invest in France Mission and Arthur Andersen, in collaboration with DATAR.)

World Investment Report 1997: Transnational Corporations, Market Structure and Competition Policy. 420 p. Sales No. E.97.II.D.10. $45.

World Investment Report 1997: Transnational Corporations, Market Structure and Competition Policy. An Overview. 70 p. Free-of-charge.

International Investment Towards the Year 2001. 81 p. Sales No. GV.E.97.0.5. $35. (Joint publication with Invest in France Mission and Arthur Andersen, in collaboration with DATAR.)

World Investment Directory. Vol. VI: West Asia 1996. 192 p. Sales No. E.97.II.A.2. $35.

World Investment Directory. Vol. V: Africa 1996. 508 p. Sales No. E.97.II.A.1. $75.

Sharing Asia's Dynamism: Asian Direct Investment in the European Union. 192 p. Sales No. E.97.II.D.1. $26.

Transnational Corporations and World Development. 656 p. ISBN
0-415-08560-8 (hardback), 0-415-08561-6 (paperback). £65 (hardback),
£20.00 (paperback). (Published by International Thomson Business
Press on behalf of UNCTAD.)

*Companies without Borders: Transnational Corporations in the
1990s.* 224 p. ISBN 0-415-12526-X. £47.50. (Published by International
Thomson Business Press on behalf of UNCTAD.)

The New Globalism and Developing Countries. 336 p. ISBN 92-
808-0944-X. $25. (Published by United Nations University Press.)

*Investing in Asia's Dynamism: European Union Direct Investment
in Asia.* 124 p. ISBN 92-827-7675-1. ECU 14. (Joint publication with
the European Commission.)

*World Investment Report 1996: Investment, Trade and International
Policy Arrangements.* 332 p. Sales No. E.96.II.A.14. $45.

*World Investment Report 1996: Investment, Trade and International
Policy Arrangements. An Overview.* 51 p. Free-of-charge.

International Investment Instruments: A Compendium. Vol. I. 371
p. Sales No. E.96.II.A.9; Vol. II. 577 p. Sales No. E.96.II.A.10; Vol.
III. 389 p. Sales No. E.96.II.A.11; the 3-volume set, Sales No. E.96.II.A.12.
$125.

*World Investment Report 1995: Transnational Corporations and
Competitiveness.* 491 p. Sales No. E.95.II.A.9. $45.

*World Investment Report 1995: Transnational Corporations and
Competitiveness. An Overview.* 51 p. Free-of-charge.

Accounting for Sustainable Forestry Management. A Case Study.
46 p. Sales No. E.94.II.A.17. $22.

*Small and Medium-sized Transnational Corporations. Executive
Summary and Report of the Osaka Conference.* 60 p. Free-of-
charge.

World Investment Report 1994: Transnational Corporations, Employment and the Workplace. 482 p. Sales No. E.94.II.A.14. $45.

World Investment Report 1994: Transnational Corporations, Employment and the Workplace. An Executive Summary. 34 p. Free-of-charge.

Liberalizing International Transactions in Services: A Handbook. 182 p. Sales No. E.94.II.A.11. $45. (Joint publication with the World Bank.)

World Investment Directory. Vol. IV: Latin America and the Caribbean. 478 p. Sales No. E.94.II.A.10. $65.

Conclusions on Accounting and Reporting by Transnational Corporations. 47 p. Sales No. E.94.II.A.9. $25.

Accounting, Valuation and Privatization. 190 p. Sales No. E.94.II.A.3. $25.

Environmental Management in Transnational Corporations: Report on the Benchmark Corporate Environment Survey. 278 p. Sales No. E.94.II.A.2. $29.95.

Management Consulting: A Survey of the Industry and Its Largest Firms. 100 p. Sales No. E.93.II.A.17. $25.

Transnational Corporations: A Selective Bibliography, 1991-1992. 736 p. Sales No. E.93.II.A.16. $75. (English/French.)

Small and Medium-sized Transnational Corporations: Role, Impact and Policy Implications. 242 p. Sales No. E.93.II.A.15. $35.

World Investment Report 1993: Transnational Corporations and Integrated International Production. 290 p. Sales No. E.93.II.A.14. $45.

World Investment Report 1993: Transnational Corporations and Integrated International Production. An Executive Summary. 31 p. ST/CTC/159. Free-of-charge.

Foreign Investment and Trade Linkages in Developing Countries.
108 p. Sales No. E.93.II.A.12. $18.

World Investment Directory 1992. Vol. III: Developed Countries.
532 p. Sales No. E.93.II.A.9. $75.

*Transnational Corporations from Developing Countries: Impact
on Their Home Countries*. 116 p. Sales No. E.93.II.A.8. $15.

Debt-Equity Swaps and Development. 150 p. Sales No. E.93.II.A.7.
$35.

*From the Common Market to EC 92: Regional Economic Integration
in the European Community and Transnational Corporations*. 134
p. Sales No. E.93.II.A.2. $25.

World Investment Directory 1992. Vol. II: Central and Eastern Europe.
432 p. Sales No. E.93.II.A.1. $65. (Joint publication with the United
Nations Economic Commission for Europe.)

The East-West Business Directory 1991/1992. 570 p. Sales No.
E.92.II.A.20. $65.

*World Investment Report 1992: Transnational Corporations as Engines
of Growth: An Executive Summary*. 30 p. Sales No. E.92.II.A.24.
Free-of-charge.

*World Investment Report 1992: Transnational Corporations as Engines
of Growth*. 356 p. Sales No. E.92.II.A.19. $45.

World Investment Directory 1992. Vol. I: Asia and the Pacific. 356
p. Sales No. E.92.II.A.11. $65.

Climate Change and Transnational Corporations: Analysis and Trends.
110 p. Sales No. E.92.II.A.7. $16.50.

Foreign Direct Investment and Transfer of Technology in India. 150
p. Sales No. E.92.II.A.3. $20.

*The Determinants of Foreign Direct Investment: A Survey of the
Evidence*. 84 p. Sales No. E.92.II.A.2. $12.50.

The Impact of Trade-Related Investment Measures on Trade and Development: Theory, Evidence and Policy Implications. 108 p. Sales No. E.91.II.A.19. $17.50. (Joint publication with the United Nations Centre on Transnational Corporations.)

Transnational Corporations and Industrial Hazards Disclosure. 98 p. Sales No. E.91.II.A.18. $17.50.

Transnational Business Information: A Manual of Needs and Sources. 216 p. Sales No. E.91.II.A.13. $45.

World Investment Report 1991: The Triad in Foreign Direct Investment. 108 p. Sales No.E.91.II.A.12. $25.

C. Serial publications

Current Studies, Series A

No. 30.   *Incentives and Foreign Direct Investment*. 98 p. Sales No. E.96.II.A.6. $30. (English/French.)

No. 29.   *Foreign Direct Investment, Trade, Aid and Migration*. 100 p. Sales No. E.96.II.A.8. $25. (Joint publication with the International Organization for Migration.)

No. 28.   *Foreign Direct Investment in Africa*. 119 p. Sales No. E.95.II.A.6. $20.

No. 27.   *Tradability of Banking Services: Impact and Implications*. 195 p. Sales No. E.94.II.A.12. $50.

No. 26.   *Explaining and Forecasting Regional Flows of Foreign Direct Investment*. 58 p. Sales No. E.94.II.A.5. $25.

No. 25.   *International Tradability in Insurance Services*. 54 p. Sales No. E.93.II.A.11. $20.

No. 24.   *Intellectual Property Rights and Foreign Direct Investment*. 108 p. Sales No. E.93.II.A.10. $20.

No. 23. *The Transnationalization of Service Industries: An Empirical Analysis of the Determinants of Foreign Direct Investment by Transnational Service Corporations*. 62 p. Sales No. E.93.II.A.3. $15.

No. 22. *Transnational Banks and the External Indebtedness of Developing Countries: Impact of Regulatory Changes*. 48 p. Sales No. E.92.II.A.10. $12.

No. 20. *Foreign Direct Investment, Debt and Home Country Policies*. 50 p. Sales No. E.90.II.A.16. $12.

No. 19. *New Issues in the Uruguay Round of Multilateral Trade Negotiations*. 52 p. Sales No. E.90.II.A.15. $12.50.

No. 18. *Foreign Direct Investment and Industrial Restructuring in Mexico*. 114 p. Sales No. E.92.II.A.9. $12.

No. 17. *Government Policies and Foreign Direct Investment*. 68 p. Sales No. E.91.II.A.20. $12.50.

The United Nations Library on Transnational Corporations
(Published by Routledge on behalf of the United Nations.)

Set A (Boxed set of 4 volumes. ISBN 0-415-08554-3. £350):
Volume One: *The Theory of Transnational Corporations*. 464 p.
Volume Two: *Transnational Corporations: A Historical Perspective*. 464 p.
Volume Three: *Transnational Corporations and Economic Development*. 448 p.
Volume Four: *Transnational Corporations and Business Strategy*. 416 p.

Set B (Boxed set of 4 volumes. ISBN 0-415-08555-1. £350):
Volume Five: *International Financial Management*. 400 p.
Volume Six: *Organization of Transnational Corporations*. 400 p.
Volume Seven: *Governments and Transnational Corporations*. 352 p.
Volume Eight: *Transnational Corporations and International Trade and Payments*. 320 p.

Set C (Boxed set of 4 volumes. ISBN 0-415-08556-X. £350):
Volume Nine: *Transnational Corporations and Regional Economic Integration*. 331 p.
Volume Ten: *Transnational Corporations and the Exploitation of Natural Resources*. 397 p.
Volume Eleven: *Transnational Corporations and Industrialization*. 425 p.
Volume Twelve: *Transnational Corporations in Services*. 437 p.

Set D (Boxed set of 4 volumes. ISBN 0-415-08557-8. £350):
Volume Thirteen: *Cooperative Forms of Transnational Corporation Activity*. 419 p.
Volume Fourteen: *Transnational Corporations: Transfer Pricing and Taxation*. 330 p.
Volume Fifteen: *Transnational Corporations: Market Structure and Industrial Performance*. 383 p.
Volume Sixteen: *Transnational Corporations and Human Resources*. 429 p.

Set E (Boxed set of 4 volumes. ISBN 0-415-08558-6. £350):
Volume Seventeen: *Transnational Corporations and Innovatory Activities*. 447 p.
Volume Eighteen: *Transnational Corporations and Technology Transfer to Developing Countries*. 486 p.
Volume Nineteen: *Transnational Corporations and National Law*. 322 p.
Volume Twenty: *Transnational Corporations: The International Legal Framework*. 545 p.

D. Journals

Transnational Corporations (formerly *The CTC Reporter*).

Published three times a year. Annual subscription price: $45; individual issues $20.

ProInvest, a quarterly newsletter, available free of charge.

United Nations publications may be obtained from bookstores and distributors throughout the world. Please consult your bookstore or write to:

United Nations Publications

Sales Section	OR	Sales Section
Room DC2-0853		United Nations Office at Geneva
United Nations Secretariat		Palais des Nations
New York, NY 10017		CH-1211 Geneva 10
U.S.A.		Switzerland
Tel: (1-212) 963-8302 or (800) 253-9646		
Tel: (41-22) 917-1234		
Fax: (1-212) 963-3489		Fax: (41-22) 917-0123
E-mail: publications@un.org		E-mail: unpubli@unorg.ch

All prices are quoted in United States dollars.
For further information on the work of the Division on Investment, Technology and Enterprise Development, UNCTAD, please address inquiries to:

United Nations Conference on Trade and Development
Division on Investment, Technology and Enterprise Development
Palais des Nations, Room E-9123
CH-1211 Geneva 10
Switzerland
Telephone: (41-22) 907-5707
Telefax: (41-22) 907-0194
E-mail: almario.medarde@unctad.org

QUESTIONNAIRE

National Treatment

Sales No. E.99.II.D.16

In order to improve the quality and relevance of the work of the UNCTAD Division on Investment, Technology and Enterprise Development, it would be useful to receive the views of readers on this and other similar publications. It would therefore be greatly appreciated if you could complete the following questionnaire and return it to:

Readership Survey
UNCTAD Division on Investment, Technology and Enterprise
Development
United Nations Office in Geneva
Palais des Nations
Room E-9123
CH-1211 Geneva 10
Switzerland
Fax: 41-22 907-0194

1. Name and address of respondent (optional):

    _____

    _____

    _____

    _____

2. Which of the following best describes your area of work?

    _____

Government ☐   Public enterprise ☐

Private enterprise   Academic or
institution ☐   research ☐

International
organization ☐   Media ☐

Not-for-profit
organization ☐   Other (specify)

3.   In which country do you work?_____

4.   What is your assessment of the contents of this publication?

Excellent ☐   Adequate ☐

Good ☐   Poor ☐

5.   How useful is this publication to your work?

Very useful ☐   Of some use ☐   Irrelevant ☐

6.   Please indicate the three things you liked best about this publication:

7.   Please indicate the three things you liked least about this publication:

8.   If you have read more than the present publication of the UNCTAD Division on Investment, Enterprise Development and Technology, what is your overall assessment of them?

Consistently good ☐ Usually good, but with some exceptions ☐

Generally mediocre ☐ Poor ☐

9.   On the average, how useful are these publications to you in your work?

Very useful ☐ Of some use ☐ Irrelevant ☐

10.   Are you a regular recipient of *Transnational Corporations* (formerly *The CTC Reporter*), the Division's tri-annual refereed journal?

Yes ☐ No ☐

If not, please check here if you would like to receive a sample copy sent to the name and address you have given above
☐

Notes

Notes

Notes

كيفية الحصول على منشورات الأمم المتحدة

يمكن الحصول على منشورات الأمم المتحدة من المكتبات ودور التوزيع في جميع أنحاء العالم. استعلم عنـها مـن
المكتبة التي تتعامل معها أو اكتب إلى: الأمم المتحدة، قسم البيع في نيويورك أو في جنيف.

如何购取联合国出版物

联合国出版物在全世界各地的书店和经售处均有发售. 请向书店询问或写信到纽约或日内瓦的联合国销售组.

HOW TO OBTAIN UNITED NATIONS PUBLICATIONS

United Nations publications may be obtained from bookstores and distributors
throughout the world. Consult your bookstore or write to: United Nations, Sales
Section, New York or Geneva.

COMMENT SE PROCURER LES PUBLICATIONS DES NATIONS UNIES

Les publications des Nations Unies sont en vente dans les librairies et les agences
dépositaires du monde entier. Informez-vous auprès de votre libraire ou adressez-
vous à : Nations Unies, Section des ventes, New York ou Genève.

КАК ПОЛУЧИТЬ ИЗДАНИЯ ОРГАНИЗАЦИИ ОБЪЕДИНЕННЫХ НАЦИЙ

Издания Организации Объединенных Наций можно купить в книжных мага-
зинах и агентствах во всех районах мира. Наводите справки об изданиях в
вашем книжном магазине или пишите по адресу: Организация Объединенных
Наций, Секция по продаже изданий, Нью-Йорк или Женева.

COMO CONSEGUIR PUBLICACIONES DE LAS NACIONES UNIDAS

Las publicaciones de las Naciones Unidas están en venta en librerías y casas distri-
buidoras en todas partes del mundo. Consulte a su librero o diríjase a: Naciones
Unidas, Sección de Ventas, Nueva York o Ginebra.

Printed at United Nations, Geneva
GE.99-52334–July 1999–5,270

United Nations publication
Sales No. E.99.II.D.16

UNCTAD/ITE/IIT/11 (Vol. IV)

ISBN 92-1-112455-7